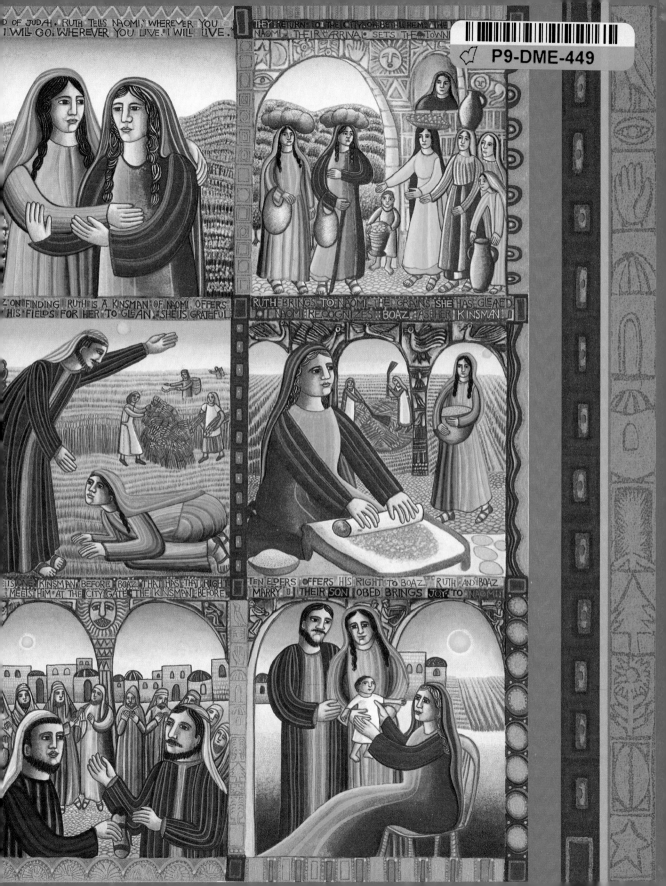

The Story of Ruth

Twelve Moments in Every Woman's Life

The Story of Ruth

Twelve Moments in Every Woman's Life

JOAN D. CHITTISTER

Art by

JOHN AUGUST SWANSON

WILLIAM B. EERDMANS PUBLISHING COMPANY

GRAND RAPIDS, MICHIGAN / CAMBRIDGE, U.K.

NOVALIS

SAINT PAUL UNIVERSITY, OTTAWA

Published jointly 2000 in the U.S.A. by
Wm B. Eerdmans Publishing Company
255 Jefferson Ave. S.E., Grand Rapids, Michigan 49503 /
P.O. Box 163, Cambridge CB3 9PU U.K.
and in Canada by
Novalis, Saint Paul University, 223 Main Street
Ottawa, Ontario K1S 1C4

Printed in the United States of America

05 04 03 02 01 00   7 6 5 4 3 2 1

Library of Congress Cataloging-in-Publication Data

Chittister, Joan D.
The story of Ruth: twelve moments in every woman's life /
Joan Chittister; art by John August Swanson
p.   cm.
Includes bibliographical references.
ISBN 0-8028-4742-0 (hardcover: alk. paper)
1. Ruth (Biblical figure). 2. Women — Religious life. I. Title.
BS1315.5.C45 2000
248.8'43 — dc21

99-086148

Canadian Cataloguing in Publication Data

Chittister, Joan D.
The Book of Ruth: twelve moments in every woman's life
ISBN 2-89507-091-1
1. Christian women-Religious life. 2. Self-actualization
(Psychology-Religious Aspects). 3. Bible. O.T. Ruth.
I. Title.
BS1315.4.C55 2000 248.8'43 C00-900288-X

Scripture quotations in this publication are from the New Revised Standard Version Bible,
copyright © 1989 by the Division of Christian Education of the National Council of
Churches of Christ in the U.S.A., and used by permission.

Book and jacket design by: Walt Matzke

Dedication

This book is dedicated to Gail
in whom lives the spirit of both Ruth and Naomi
and because of whom I am mindful of the marrow of each always.

Joan D. Chittister

My interest in painting "stories" or narrative art comes from my mother's family
accounts of their leaving Mexico during the revolutionary times. Her stories of
compassion, heroism, and sacrifice help me remember my immigrant roots. I dedicate
this book to her, Magdalena Velasquez Swanson, born in 1909 in Chihuahua, Mexico.

The inspiration for my art for *The Story of Ruth* is the refugees, immigrants,
and cultural groups who move throughout the earth in history, seeking a place
to live in peace and dignity. Their stories continue and connect us to the journey
of Ruth and Naomi.

Another person who encouraged me to work on this theme is my pastor,
Fr. Michael McFadden, O.S.A., who spent several years in Latin America working
in U.N. refugee camps. His stories of these refugees helped me understand the
courage, hope, and strength that are part of the journey and story of the
refugees Ruth and Naomi.

John August Swanson

Contents

Acknowledgments

In the final analysis, the biblical women Ruth and Naomi are simply metaphors, models of all the women of the world who push and prod and guide and give support to the rest of us through all the trying moments of life, however momentous, however mundane.

Each of us can look back on the women who were Naomis for us — older women because of whom our lives were changed. Each of us remembers with concern — with pride — the young Ruths in our lives who poised to take one step and then, despite our best advice, took what became for both our sakes an even better one.

The Ruths and Naomis of the human estate make the world go round. No one of us can get through the phases of our separate flowerings without their promptings. Without them growth is static, the worst happens, all of life's inevitables look impossible. The Ruths and Naomis of the world take the measure of what we think we cannot surmount alone and show us that it is vincible.

This small book, too, has known all those stages but, thanks to the Ruths and Naomis of my own life, has come to being, regardless of all obstacles. I am deeply aware of both the spirit and the quality they brought to this work. No amount of acknowledgment can begin to convey either its meaning to me as a person or its real impact on the text.

I am grateful to Sandra de Groot, my editor, who in the process of reflecting with me about this work as a woman, as a professional, has become a sister as well.

I am grateful to those who gave their time to read and measure this work against their own life experiences: to Dorothy Stoner, OSB; Mary Hembrow Snyder; Anne McCarthy, OSB; Gail Grossman Freyne; Linda Romey, OSB; Kathleen Stephens; Mary Louise St. John, OSB; Brother Tomas Bezanzon; Maureen Tobin, OSB; Mary Lou Kownaci, OSB; and Christine Vladimiroff, OSB. They have given flesh to its truths and depth to its insights.

I am especially grateful to those who worked through the manuscript with me a word at a time, a day at a time, until the final period. Marlene Bertke, OSB; Linda Romey, OSB; and

Mary Lee Farrell, GNSH, tested every sentence, every idea, to the ultimate. And then they tested it again.

I never stop being grateful to Maureen Tobin, OSB, a Naomi in truth, who brings the strength and the strategy it takes to get a book written and go on living at the same time.

I remain forever grateful to Bill and Betsy Vorscheck, longtime friends, open-hearted companions, who consistently provide me the space and the time it takes to sit and wait for the words to bring life to the ideas.

Having been committed to *The Story of Ruth* for years, I'm grateful for John August Swanson for bringing it to life with the kind of artistic insight and quality that ground these reflections in stark beauty.

Finally, I am grateful to all of those women in my life who have been either Naomi or Ruth to me. Thanks to you, I have been able to risk the nights and welcome the dawn.

Joan D. Chittister

Artist's Notes

In the spring of 1990, I began to study the biblical Book of Ruth, seeking the episodes in the story that could be the most visual. The preliminary sketches and drawings developed into a series of miniatures. As I developed the drawings, I decided to unify the twelve panels of the artwork. I arranged the design so that there are three rows of four panels — the panels in each of these rows have the same horizon line. The first row has a connecting line with the hills. The second row has a connecting line with the barley fields. The third uses the horizon line along with incorporating architectural arches to frame the panels. In the collected miniature panels of *The Story of Ruth*, I was able to portray a more complete narrative than I would have by relying on only one large scene. This use of the narrative in multi-panels has a connection to ancient and medieval art. I was inspired to create the same intensity and concentration that I found in Byzantine icons and the miniatures found in medieval illuminated manuscripts.

In the late summer, I completed the watercolor painting. When exhibited, it moved many people. It was then that I began to consider developing it into a hand-printed limited-edition serigraph. I would be the publisher. I began the phone calls and correspondence to schedule the publishing of *The Story of Ruth,* and began to work with the printers at Advanced Graphics Studio in London in the spring of 1991.

At the studio we planned all technical phases of the printing. I decided to print the serigraph with an image size of 27½″ x 34¼″ (larger than the original watercolor painting). To create the serigraph, I planned the sequence of the colors and used many glazes of transparent inks to saturate each of the panels with warm, rich colors and patterns. I drew a stencil for each of the 48 colors printed. For the decorative borders, I layered various printings of metallic gold inks to add embellishments and designs. Above each panel I drew and printed the lettering for the accompanying text with bright colors. I am happy with the result of spending many months to print the serigraph *The Story of Ruth.*

Now Joan Chittister and I — she as writer and I as artist — have merged our creative energies to retell this ancient biblical story. This has been for me an exciting collaboration. Joan is a prophetic voice asking us to look and understand this poignant and powerful story with its relation to lives today around the world.

This is not only a women's book — we all can learn from Joan's reflections on Ruth's story. I hope men will see it as an opportunity to grow in awareness and sensitivity. There is a healing that takes place when someone accompanies another on life's journey, especially when this journey is filled with struggles. In the story of Ruth and Naomi, we see hope emerge out of loss and tragedy.

This is a book that can empower each of us. It is a way to look at our own stories and appreciate them better. Then we can "accompany"; then we can be part of the journey with others — women, refugees, and the poor. For the story of Ruth is a universal story of the poor, the marginalized, and the refugee. This story gave me an insight into the struggles and lives of our universal human family, all our ancient ancestors, and the lives of all our families. For me, *The Story of Ruth* opens my heart to see generosity and compassion that still transcends history and peoples. It is a story from which we still have much to learn.

John August Swanson

Ruth and Naomi: Your Story and Mine

The Book of Ruth is a woman's story about a woman's life. Written thousands of years ago — anywhere from 500 to 1000 B.C.E., depending on which linguistic clues we choose to follow — it is, nevertheless, a perennial. Composed, faith tells us, under the inspiration of the Divine, it calls us to reflect in every generation on what it means to be a whole woman, a spiritual woman, yet today. It models what every woman alive lives still. It is an icon of what it means to be a woman of God, to live under the impulse of the Spirit, to be a creative part of God's creative power. One moment at a time it takes us from one life moment to another to show us how God works in us all, to remind us to what God calls us all, whatever the period, whatever the place. It is a silhouette of every woman's life frozen in time and held up for reflection.

Life, it seems to me in retrospect, is only incidentally made up of chronological pieces specific to this person in this place at this time. Instead, life, its substance and meaning, is really made up of a series of defining moments — moments of loss, risk, change, transformation, relationship, and survival — that mark every woman's passage through time in a way separate from the men around her and that shape her as she goes. All of them stand stark and unadorned in Ruth, pared to the marrow and clear in their challenges. The way we deal with each of these moments determines who and what we really are, who and what we are intended to be, who and what we can become both spiritually and socially.

The Scriptures call it the Book of Ruth. I am not convinced of the full truth of the title. It is at least the Book of Ruth and Naomi, and maybe, actually, The Book of Naomi, the older, wiser woman who having lived through one kind of life wants a better one for Ruth. The younger woman, Naomi knows, looks up to her as model and mentor and friend, and will follow in her footsteps. But which footsteps and how if she is to be everything God wants her to be?

The story as it's told is a simple one: It is the story of two women — one old, one young — both childless and vulnerable, both marginal to the systems around them — who find themselves dealing with limited resources, deep pain, a hostile world, and great concern for the situation of the other. It's a familiar situation for most women yet today who find themselves left to survive in a system to which they do not have full access. Naomi's husband has died — and now ten years later, her two sons, as well. Naomi is left alone in Moab now, the foreign land to which the family, years before, had immigrated in order to escape famine at home. She has no real roots there, no long-time friends to see her through the kind of loss that turns lonely lives back upon themselves, only two Moabite daughters-in-law.

Elimelech, Naomi's deceased husband, had moved the family from Bethlehem, the city of their birth, to this other one where they were outsiders, come-latelies to the social scene, in search of the economic security that an agriculture in decline back home could not promise. It was good short-term thinking, perhaps, if you were the bread winner in the family, but for Naomi, the now widowed wife in an alien land, it spelled long-term disaster. To leave her foreign home for the open road is risky for Naomi as a woman alone, but to stay where she is means sure destitution. An outlander in a system that made no provision for widows, Naomi decides when the last man in the family dies to return to Bethlehem, her homeland. There, she will at least have some old social ties and there may even yet be remnants of her family, however distant the relationships.

Naomi's daughters-in-law, Ruth and Orpah, are now, like herself, single women, widows, in a world where not to be attached to a man is to be in danger, socially, economically, and physically. Ruth and Orpah are, then, faced with a major decision: to cling to what they are where they are or to become new women in a new world. Ruth and Orpah, unlike Naomi, are young enough to simply begin the old pattern all over again — to marry, settle down where they've always been, have children, go on maintaining the society around them as their mothers and grandmothers have done for centuries. Or they can seize this moment in life to become someone new, to start again alone and in a place other than their beginnings. They can take what appears as God's one and only will for them or they can stretch themselves to the limits of themselves to find the God who waits for them in what they have yet to become.

What woman has not faced the question of what it would mean to strike out on a different course than the one defined for her by time and the society in which she lives? What unmarried woman, let alone a widow, does not know the implications of the situation even yet? Life for the single woman is far different than life for the single man. There are few, if any, single friends for a single woman to relate to in a social world made up of couples, and the single woman is often seen as a threat. There are sparse assets to draw on for the rest of life when a woman has no job or cannot get one that pays enough to support the present and provide for the future at the same time because she is a woman. And, as any widow — any woman — knows, there is some kind of danger, physical or material, everywhere for the unmarried woman.

One daughter-in-law, Orpah — the sensible one, many would say — decides to stay in Moab, her homeland, where the chances of another marriage are presumably better than they would be in a strange place. Orpah will simply marry again and go on as usual. It's an honorable choice and a safe one. It clings to what is, in the hope that it can be good again.

Ruth, on the other hand, the second daughter-in-law, decides to go with Naomi to a land where she will be an eternal outsider and where the national prejudice against Moabites, let alone single Moabite women, goes deep. It is a very precarious situation for a young woman. Interracial marriages are frowned upon in early Israel, and a woman without a husband in a culture where a woman's social security depends on her being linked to a man is a sorry sight. But Ruth makes the bold choice, the one filled with faith that the God of yesterday is also the God of today, that the God who took one thing away has something else in store for her. Ruth opts to begin again somewhere else in very new ways, whatever the odds against her. She determines to follow a God who worked through Miriam, Rachel, Sarah and Leah as well as through Moses, Jacob and Abraham to save a world and lead a people.

The book of Naomi and Ruth, therefore, is the story of three women left to fend for themselves in a world geared to the autonomy and ability of men but not to the freedom and full development of women. It is the story of what it takes to discover the God within. It is a defining moment for all three.

In fact, there are delineating moments in every human life, points after which we are never quite the same again. Perhaps especially for women they are often intensely private, deeply personal ones. What these three women do in the midst of their own struggles — how they thread their way through the system as women, what qualities it takes, and what decisions it requires as they do — is model enough for anyone, but for women in a special way. Even now. Even here.

Most women live very unpretentious lives. We grow up, work hard, take care of families, stumble through relationships, endure losses, and, in the course of it, contend, too often all alone, with the complexities that come from trying to balance the values of the world around us with what our own experiences and talents and wisdom dictate. It is not an easy task, for either men or women, of course. The problem is that there is a dimension to a woman's life that is unique to being a woman. Women live in two worlds — one private, one public — but, if truth were known, are by and large considered native to only one of them. What we know in the private arena is seldom considered common coin in the other.

Women now commonly function on the edge of two systems, one public and one private. We stand with a foot in both worlds, one that promises us home and hearth for obeying the social roles of the culture, one that requires us to shoulder our private worlds and sustain our public ones at the same time but without guarantee of the means to do either. The woman called by God, either by life circumstance or by personal gift, to live in both knows the expense to the self of following the call.

Often denied equal pay and pension benefits, for instance, most women live with fewer resources than most of the men around them. Defined as the primary caretakers of humanity, they labor under more limited professional opportunities than men and so must deal with the lack of personal and financial security such restrictions imply in a highly professional world. Full of intelligence and heart and creativity, they struggle almost reflexively to become what they know themselves to be despite the odds against them. And, ironically, impelled, if for no other reason than economic ones, to function both inside and outside the home, women carry responsibilities far beyond the strength of the average person to bear. They care for small children, look after old relatives, maintain busy homes, work the eight-hour day for essential resources, manage the greater part of the housework, and all the while try to become whole persons themselves by pursuing the development of their own potential and dreaming their own dreams. All the while they look for spiritual models to show them the way.

Far too often for far too many, however, life lived on such a flimsy bridge of hope and chance, of strain and burden, begins to sway and slip. A marriage crumbles, a husband leaves, a job ends, a career vanishes, the money runs out but the costs do not. There are few role models in the history of the world for a woman to refer to when one end or the other of these very fragmented lives sags or snaps. It is precisely then that the story of Ruth and Naomi begins to matter. In the Book of Ruth, the Word of God takes a position on women that defies the social tradition, in this day as well as in that one. In the Book of Ruth, God calls us beyond the stereotypes and the social barriers to fullness of life and wholeness of being. It is a spiritual journey meant clearly for us all.

Naomi and Ruth have something to say to each of us, even yet, even now as we face loss and change and risk and the unfamiliar in our own lives and the eternal debate over God's will for women. The Book of Ruth is a treatise on the spirituality of womanhood. John August Swanson paints the scenes; you and I live them. But how? And with what effect on our hoping hearts, our seared souls, our psyches, our world?

Chapter One Loss

NAOMI AND HER TWO DAUGHTERS-IN-LAW, ORPAH AND RUTH HAVE LOST AND BURIED THEIR HUSBANDS, THEY LEAVE THE LAND OF MOAB

Ruth 1:1   In the days when the judges ruled, there was a famine in the land; and Elimelech, a man of Bethlehem in Judah, with his wife and two sons went to reside in the country of Moab. . . . Elimelech, Naomi's husband, died, and she was left with her two sons. They married Moabite women. . . . Then the two sons also died.

The Book of Ruth begins in tragedy. Three women are left with three dead husbands and no means of support. It is a crossover moment in time. It is the moment that leads these women — and we ourselves, perhaps — to God's new time.

Moments of great loss throw a woman back on her own assets. With little in the way of external resources to barter — money, social connections, education — it is what a woman is inside herself that will have to count. It is her faith in the ultimate logic of God in her life that is her only real resource. Naomi, Ruth, and Orpah are women coping with loss. Like most women in the world even today, the lives of Naomi and her daughters-in-law are tied to the fortunes of the men whose work and position have shaped their worlds. They have lost the men in their lives and, with the men, their social status and economic security as well. What happens to them now rests entirely on them and their trust in the fullness of their own creation. It is a moment of deep spiritual revelation.

Naomi is an old woman without assets. Ruth and Orpah are young women with sparse options. They can try to find a man to support them, if they're lucky, or they can remain widows and throw themselves on the grudging mercy of the community at large. Naomi and Ruth and Orpah are alone in the world now. They have only one another. And God.

Like everyone ever born who goes through sudden, defining loss of any kind, these women find themselves faced with the question: Who am I when I am no longer who and what I was? Like the rest of us for whom the very foundations of our lives are given to shifting from day to day, there are no miracles in sight to save them, no angels on the road to point the way. Nothing. Everything they had, everything they ever thought they wanted, is gone. There are no anchors to steady them, no safety nets to catch them. Now they have only themselves on which to depend. Only the Spirit of God to lead them on through a world that has little place for them at all.

Women everywhere know the feeling, have felt the helplessness that attends abandonment and marginalization. Women know what it's like to be the eternal outsider looking in. Women know the sense of powerlessness that comes from being only a woman in a world shaped primarily for men. What can possibly be the will of God for a woman at a time like this? What does God have in mind for women when it seems that the world has little or nothing in mind for women at all — once motherhood ends, or there is no man to support them, or there is no institution to define them, or there is no one and nothing whose need legitimates their existence? In the Book of Ruth, God takes a stand on the side of the woman alone in the world. In the Book of Ruth, God pronounces her whole and capable of her own direction.

There is a difference between great misfortune and great loss. Misfortune is a temporary detour through a jungle of opportunities. It is a case of "If not this, then that." "If I can't get to medical school, then I'll be a lawyer." "If I can't own a farm, I'll work on one." When my young father died, my twenty-one-year-old mother had nowhere to go, no professional education to fall back on, no place in the circle of men who did the hiring, opened the businesses, controlled the credit in town. Institutions did not invest in women. Thirty years later when her second husband, my stepfather, died as well, little had really changed. She still had few options. She was still a woman in a society of male organizations. She still had only what his job enabled him to leave her to live on. Today, over half the national workforce are women, but over 80 percent of them are employed only in the service industries, where wages are low and benefits are nil. If women earned what men earn, current studies show, the national poverty rate would be cut in half.[1] For these women, too, losing the men in their lives is still to be left on the brink of destitution.

Clearly, women left to fend for themselves in this world even today do not have great "misfortunes"; they have life-changing losses. God, it seems, leads them down dark roads from which there is no dignified egress, little hope of earthly salvation. But God, the Book of Ruth is clear, has more in mind for them than that.

Loss, any kind of loss — rejection, abandonment, divorce, death — is a shocking, numbing, gray thing that at the outset, at least, freezes the heart and slows the mind. Loss changes life at the root. Irrevocably. What was once the center of life — the person, the position, the plan, the lifestyle — is no more. What shaped our identities, what fashioned our days and filled our sleep, what gave us meaning and direction, comfort and support, has disappeared like sunset on a cloudless night. And with the loss, time stands still; thought stops in mid-configuration. Life is never the same again. What we have known, almost unconsciously, often for years, to be good — to be at least familiar, sure, certain — is gone, snatched away without warning. Vanished, and without our permission. Withdrawn, and with nothing in its place.

For no acceptable reason, loss destabilizes even the most sophisticated of us, spilling us off the carousel of commonplaces we thought would never end. With little warning, with less compensation, we find ourselves left to cope with an abandoned pattern of happy yesterdays left spinning in a blur of bleak tomorrows.

It is the habitual that dies with every death, the comfortable that dissolves with every ebb and loss of the familiar. What we took for granted, what has been the unquestioned gravity of our existence, shifts and tilts and weakens. Emptiness becomes our new companion, God more a rumor than a fact. Even our spiritual certainties can fade a little: Where is God now when our world is tilting and tipping and we are left in a sea of disorientation?

To be left without the mainstay of a life is to be plunged into questioning the rest of it. To what end is life without this position, this support, this thing, this person? To what purpose is a future that has no living past? The tomorrow that, once a given, now has no design? The hope that has gone to dust, the prospect turned to mist? What can possibly be left to live for, even though, for whatever reason, live we must? Where is the will of God for us in loss?

And yet loss, once reckoned, once absorbed, is a precious gift. No, I cannot be what I was before but I can be — I must be — something new. There is

more of God in me, I discover in emptiness, than I have ever known in what I once took to be fullness.

There are spiritual lessons to be learned from loss that can be barely divined by any other means and often despite ourselves. We learn, just when we think we have nothing, just when it feels that we have not one good thing left in the world, that what we do still have is ourselves. We have, deep down inside us what no one can take away, what can never be lost either to time or to chance: We have the self that brought us to this point — and more. We have gifts of God in abundance, never noticed, never touched, perhaps, but a breath in us nevertheless and waiting to be tapped. And more, whatever we have developed over the years in the center of ourselves — the grit; the hope; the calm; the bottomless, pulsating, irrepressible trust in the providence of God despite the turns of fortune — is here now to be mined like gold, scratched out and melted down, shaped and shined into a whole new life. We have within us the raw material of life. And we have it for the taking.

Sometimes only loss releases the wealth of the accumulated self. Sometimes only loss requires the concentration of spirit that brings us to our best. Often it is only loss that reduces us to our most meaningful resource, ourselves.

Left without the security of the past, we are forced to stand alone, to find inside ourselves the steel of spirit it takes to survive the unbearable, to trust that the God who made us for life stand by — even at what feels, in the midst of loss, like the boundaries of death.

We learn that loss is simply the invitation to begin another life, to take on the rest of life, to develop the fullness of the godlife within us. In fact, loss propels us into another life whether we want to begin again or not. It's when we allow ourselves to get stuck in the quicksand of loss that we can't function, that the godly gift of loss escapes us.

Loss, ironically enough, is the catalyst of newness, a doorway to other parts of the soul, where what lies dormant in us comes alive because come alive it must. Without a capacity for the unexplored, life dies. Ironically enough, when all is said and done, we discover that what loss really leaves us with is beginnings.

To lose one phase of life is an end only to the degree that it forces us to muster our energies and turn our directions. Life is not one path; it is many paths, most of them unexplored in favor of closer, clearer ones. But when loss comes, our creating God comes to us in new and demanding ways so that we can finish the creation that has been begun in us.

Loss is not an easy road to walk, of course. One aspect of the grace of loss is grief; the other, reassessment of the past. Both are essential dimensions of the project. Unless we allow ourselves to grieve the loss, to admit its effects on our own lives, our own souls, we cannot make good decisions in the future. We will spend our lives trying to make up for the loss of something for which there is no substitute.

On the other hand, unless we begin to reassess the past, we cannot know who we were in whole before we became the thing we've lost. We will never know the full measure of what we have to bring to the rest of life. We will never know what more there is in us of God's creative energy which, long ago, has been forgotten.

Grief alone can paralyze, true, but too soon a rush to reassessment can abort the process of readiness for the future. Only grieving can release us from grief. There is no moving on to new life until we have faced the loss of the past one. And that takes time. It takes time to deal with the anger that comes from loss and which no amount of false consolations or irritating solutions — the gifts of the glib — can relieve. It takes time to absorb the shock of losing. It takes time to regain perspective. It takes time to see ourselves as separate from what we've lost. It takes time to know that being where we've been is still a gift even when we are no longer there. It takes time to see the end of something precious as the beginning of some other kind of good. It takes time to see the hand of God in the depths of darkness.

It is only when we have celebrated the gift of what we've lost that we are really ready to move on with life, to move beyond what has been to what can be, to let go. Anything else is mere survival, the grinding out of days without delight and without expectation.

Grief has a place in life. It consecrates the past to its place in memory. What we do not grieve was surely not worth having to begin with. The measure of the pain grief gives us is the measure of the love we've had.

But grief does more than memorialize what was. It also frees us for the future by giving closure to the past. It is a launching pad for possibility that legitimates questions we never thought we'd ask before we knew the shock of loss. We can ask ourselves now what were the implications of what we did before this. We can ask what it is of ourselves which, having chosen to do one thing, made other choices impossible. We can ask what it is in us that lies unfinished and begging to be done if the will of God is ever to be completed in us.

We must find what is missing in us and pursue it. We must reassess the es-sential elements of who and what we are. We must remember how it is that we first defined ourselves — independently of anything or anyone else that has defined us since. We must ask ourselves what is left in us, with these things gone, to become.

Naomi did what we all must do, one way or another, at a time of loss. Naomi, the Book of Ruth implies, went back to Bethlehem, not so much to find refuge in a family that was not there, but to be what she herself needed to be, a Hebrew, a Judean, an independent woman in the bosom of a culture she had lost years ago before its time. Naomi went back to become what else she was besides the wife of Elimelech, the mother of Mahlon and Chilion, "the leftover piece" — as the He-brew word for widow, *almānâ*, calls it — of someone else's life.[2] She went back to become herself again.

For most women anywhere, even now in fact, loss takes on a special char-acter. Women the world over have lim-ited control of the world around them. They are commonly at the mercy of the social mores in which they live. They or-dinarily have access to fewer resources, either economic or political. They bear more rigid role definitions. They have fewer options because less money always means fewer options. In Naomi we see clearly that, if Creation goes on creating in us all our lives, then the function of loss is to bring us all back to the completion of ourselves just when it seems that there is nothing left in us to develop. No one is one thing only. We are all a medley of possible beginnings, all of them straining toward fulfillment. The pain of loss lies in the fact that we so seldom realize the fullness of ourselves until the rest of life lies open in the ashes of the past. When loss finally happens, as loss inevitably will, then we get the opportunity to say either yes or no to the other parts of creation in ourselves.

The truth of loss is a freeing one: It is the grave of something we loved —

this person, this path, this place — that calls forth the resurrection of the self. Then the past has done its doing. Then the Word of God becomes new life to us. Then life becomes a series of possibilities which, when taken seriously, make us whole. Then, with Naomi, we take another road, not because we know what will happen at the end of it but because we cannot be whole without walking it. There is no doubt about it: to live the rest of life, like Naomi, bury Elimelech we must.

Chapter Two Change

NAOMI URGES HER TWO DAUGHTERS IN-LAW TO RETURN TO THEIR PARENTS HOMES, AS SHE WOULD RETURN TO THE

Ruth 1:6-7   . . . In the country of Moab, Naomi had heard that the LORD had taken note of his people and given them food. Accompanied by her two daughters-in-law, she left the place where she had been living; and they set out on the road back to Judah."

Confronted with the consequences of loss, Naomi, Ruth, and Orpah face great changes in their lives. They can do everything possible to minimize them, to deny them, to ignore them, or they can see them for what they are: God's invitations to development.

Change and loss, it must be realized, are two different things. Loss takes something away from life. Change adds something to it. Loss is a black well; change is a fork in the road. Loss is not an option; it is a necessary and inevitable part of life. Change, on the other hand, is only a possibility. It can be resisted or embraced. It can be seen as temptation or as grace. It can be borne reluctantly or it can be chosen.

A moment of change leaves a woman, in a special way, at the mercy of her circumstances, unless of course she takes it in, is open to it, sees it as simply another step in the unfolding of the self. Then she leaves herself open to works of God in her soul, the likes of which she never dreamed. Without faith in the God of change, we doom ourselves to the banality of the partial. We become one-dimensional people in a three-dimensional world. We believe in God but we do not believe that God is anywhere other than where we ourselves allow God to be. But life, God, spiritual development, is far more complex than that.

Life is a mosaic. Our years are made up of tiny, interlocking parts. Move one piece in a mosaic and nothing is exactly what it was before. Change the color, the size, the placement of any one of the pieces and the whole picture changes. Add the smallest piece to any aesthetic whole and the piece alters, if only so slightly. Something once part of the way the composition went together is missing now. Something has profaned its original integrity. Something is out of balance. Something new is to be reckoned with. No matter how fine everything else around the new piece seems yet to be, no matter how fine the new piece itself, something of the whole has gone askew, has a gap in it, is wanting.

In the Book of Ruth, one piece — death — changes the picture entirely. For Naomi, the pieces that took her to Moab, held her there, seemed to plant her there forever — her husband and their two sons — are all gone now. Life is in flux whether she wants it to be or not. She is on her way to somewhere else. She is the same person who went to Moab — but at the same time she is not. The woman who went to Moab now opts to leave it, not because she planned it that way, but because nothing else was possible for a foreign widow in a society that did not provide for foreign widows. The journey itself has transformed her from wandering wife to wandering widow. Raw but subtle change has come. She is certainly still "Naomi," but she is also certainly not. She is not the Naomi who went to Moab. She is a Naomi in process.

"Willed change," the Sufi say, "is not real. Only unwilled change is real."[3] Only unwilled change catapults us into what we did not plan to do. Only unwilled change really matters to the molding of the soul, to the stretching of the self beyond the self, in other words. And matter it does. Deeply. Willed change is what I seek and shape. Unwilled change is what seeks and reshapes me.

Change is part of every life, true. But the changes that come just from the routine of living, just from the luxury of having lived long enough to see the seasons turn, the changes that come with progressive stages of life — graduating from school, getting married, having the baby, buying the house — have the ring of commonplace to them. These are not changes that come with the exploration and discovery periods of the human condition.

Change that is real is different. These are the changes that come from life's discontinuities: Corporate downsizing happens, and the work that gave every day's rising a purpose greater than itself ends. The children move miles away suddenly to begin their own lives, and ours, as a result, takes on another flavor.

We become ill and the house we lived in for thirty years is sold in favor of the smaller, less expensive, less demanding apartment. The position I wanted and was sure to get goes to someone else, and I am left to adjust or leave. Family members most important in our own development begin to die, a favorite uncle here, a close cousin there, a sister, the partner of my heart. Real change is change that is out of my control.

The change process may be a normal one but it is a painful one regardless. When I was ten years old, we were moved without warning from one city to another. Young as I was, the ground shook under my feet. My friends were gone. My future as I had known it was gone. I could no longer be sure what tomorrow would look like. I no longer had a set of special moments to wait for, no memories to relive, no familiar faces to count on in the crowd. The world went askew, and we were never again as a family who I thought we would be. Unwilled change, indeed, takes its toll however promising, however good it may show itself to be in the long run.

The spiritual offshoot of discontinuity, however, is evolution. It grows us. It cracks us open to God in whole new ways. Creation goes on creating in us. Given new horizons, we become new people. We do things we've never done before. We begin to see things we've never seen before. We think new thoughts and dream new dreams. All the old barriers, all the old absolutes fall. We begin, if we do not cling to the past, to do what could never be done in other circumstances because those circumstances no longer bind us to the past. We begin to walk away from one life toward another, from one self to another, from one way of being in the world to another. We bloom again.

But not all of us. Some people take charge of their environment at times of change; they reach down into themselves to release an energy long untapped and rouse themselves into whole new worlds. Others cower in the corners of the past, withdraw from the outer world, accommodate, and scrape life out one day at a time. Indeed, change is a demarcating decision.

All change is not progress. What people do at times of change becomes the mark of their mettle. All change is not negotiated easily. Faced with a life that is unrefined and strange, anything can happen to the soul of a person. Some people, in fact, faced with the demands of change, change for the worst. They become drug dependent. They develop eating disorders. They go into low-grade depressions from which they never fully rise. The thought of living differently is beyond them. But other people, the Naomis of life, know in the center of

their souls that however painful the process, the only response to the God of life is life. They know that every new day in every new place is a new glimpse of the face of God. They come to understand that we live in the womb of the God who is changeless, whatever the maelstrom in which we find ourselves.

We are all people who think ourselves to be steady and then one day find ourselves in flux. We are all Naomis on the way from the grave, all Orpahs on the way to security, all Ruths on the way to a strange tomorrow.

The great spiritual question, then, becomes what to do when change comes demanding courage and finds us shivering in the cubbyhole of our souls, sure that life changed is life ended. The answer may, in the end, depend less on raw risk and more on the realization that change is a quality of growth. Real risk is not motion for its own sake. "To live is to change," John Henry Newman wrote, "and to be perfect is to have changed often."[4] Real risk is a gamble on the unfinished self, then, on what God gave us to begin with but has only now required of us in full. It is, in fact, more often than not, the interrupted past that most dictates the undefined future. It is the opportunity to become what we have always been but have never done.

Change points are those moments in life at which we get inside ourselves to find that we are not, at the end, really one person at all. We are many — each of them lying in wait to come to life. We are each a composite of experiences and abilities, of possibilities and hopes, of memories and wonder, of gifts and wishes. Every stage of life calls on a different dimension of the self. Every stage of life is another grace of being that teaches us something new about ourselves, that demands something sterner of ourselves, that enables us to learn something deeper about our God. At one stage of life, we rely on personality; at another on our skill; at a third on a latent love of adventure; at others on imagination; at others on faith. And like Naomi, as each stage spells itself out, we go back into the home of the heart to find the untapped part of the self whose life depends on the choices and changes we make now.

Change may frighten us, of course, but it may just as surely free us from our old selves and freshen us for life newborn. Change dusts off our possibilities and explodes us into new beginnings. Like Naomi and the daughters-in-law, it points us up the road of reflection, where face-to-face with ourselves, our roots, our hopes, the unanswered questions of our lives as well as the inscrutable, immovable circumstances that surround us, we begin the walk to nowhere with somewhere primal in mind. And the mosaic called life shifts again as we pilgrim it, awake to possibility as we have not been for ages and attuned to the God who beckons, who companions us, on the way.

Chapter Three Transformation

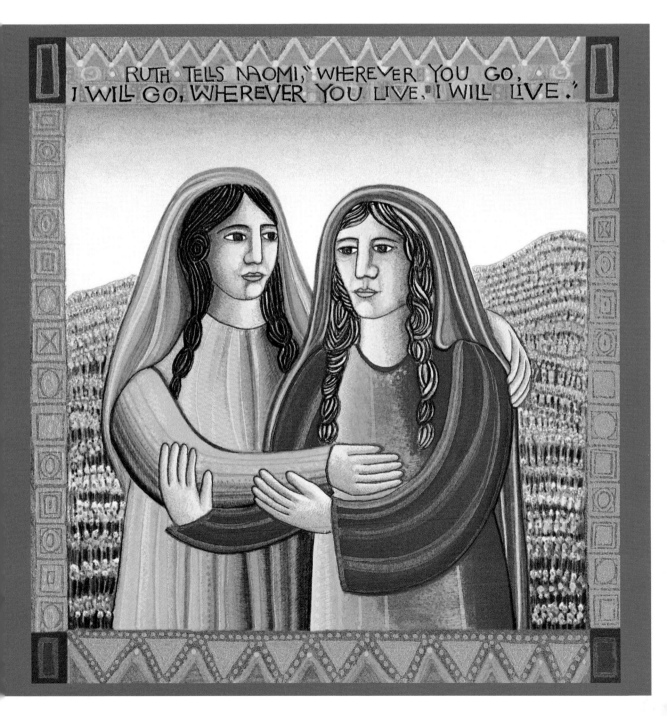

RUTH TELLS NAOMI, "WHEREVER YOU GO, I WILL GO, WHEREVER YOU LIVE, I WILL LIVE."

Ruth 1:8-9,14-17   But Naomi said to her two daughters-in-law, "Go back each of you to your mother's house. May the LORD deal kindly with you, as you have dealt with the dead and with me. The LORD grant that you may find security, each of you in the house of your husband." Then she kissed them, and they wept aloud. . . .

Orpah kissed her mother-in-law, but Ruth clung to her.

So she said, "See, your sister-in-law has gone back to her people and to her gods; return after your sister-in-law.

"But Ruth said, "Do not press me to leave you or to turn back from following you! Where you go, I will go; where you lodge, I will lodge; your people shall be my people, and your God my God. Where you die, I will die — there will I be buried. May the LORD do thus and so to me, and more as well, if even death parts me from you!"

A moment of transformation comes when something inside us shifts and, despite ourselves, we find that we are no longer the person we used to be. Then, like Naomi and Ruth we find not only that life has changed but that we have changed. Then we know with certainty that God is working in our soul.

Life, it takes a great deal of living to discover, is not static. The problem with the way we go about life is that we are too often deluded into believing that it should be one long straight road from birth to death. The world teaches us to assume that, once "settled" — once married, or graduated, or installed in what society calls a decent job — tomorrow will simply be yesterday done more, done better, done longer, done over and over again. The goal of life in this scenario is to decide early what we want to do and then to do it forever.

We're surprised, then, shocked perhaps, when after a series of satisfied yesterdays we find that we are no longer who we used to be. We find, suddenly or subtly, that yesterday is no longer the measure of our meaning, the height of our contentment, the standard of the self. Yesterday does not attract us anymore. What we did before, what we are doing now, we come to realize, simply does not fit any longer. It does not challenge, it does not fulfill, it does not give

life the kind of light it takes to lure it on. What we believed yesterday — about life, about ourselves, about the world around us — we no longer hold. The person we knew ourselves to be when we began the journey has turned into someone else. And suddenly, for no apparent reason, the journey once so bright and sure turns to dust.

It is a common consciousness. It touches everyone, everywhere. After almost twenty years of religious life, little by little I began to discover that what had made sense to me in the past, what had seemed to me to be essential to a formal religious commitment — long medieval dresses and veils, childlike obedience, passive acceptance of social customs from long past — no longer gave substance to life, no longer made sense of living, no longer spoke to me of God. Suddenly, I was lost amid the shards of the past with no clear destination in sight. I had only the sure certainty that where we were now as religious, as women, we had to leave if God was to be born anew in us in this time and this place.

They are not comfortable moments, these glimpses beyond the now. They feel like infidelity. But they taste like life.

Transformation is not happenstance; it is a revolution of the soul. Doing something over and over, being somewhere again and again, saying yes and yes and yes to what we said yes to before, we find, is suddenly no answer to the questions of today for us. We stop being whoever it was who began this journey. We are not now who we were. We don't want any longer to be who everyone thinks we're supposed to be. Our souls stretch to the bursting point and home becomes foreign soil. Somehow, without ever knowing that it happened, we awake to find ourselves transformed. "You're not the woman I married," he says. "You're acting silly," our best friends say. "You can't be serious?" the family says. "You're not a real nun," the traditionalists say. It is a solemn and sober moment. It is Passover time. Something is dying and something is coming to life.

The question, of course, is what to do with these new questions, these old dissatisfactions, these upstart doubts. Swallow them back into the depths of the self, let them out a little at a time like steam out of a kettle, or risk the sweet lunacy of following them to the end, of embracing them, of going where they lead in the hope that the God who signals this journey for us will be there at its end? Safety lies on one hand, possible shipwreck on the other. Both of them, if unattended, are deadly to the soul. If I stay where I am and all my past life learnings lie at waste, I die before my time. If I leave where I am, but

my new questions are bogus, my call to new life nothing but a sham, I die in disgrace. It is indeed the crossroads of the soul. God stands in the dark of it, waiting for me to become the rest of me.

Ruth and Orpah, the daughters-in-law of the old widow Naomi, find themselves at a juncture of life which they did not choose and for which they are not prepared. There is a choice to be made: they must either let Naomi go on to Bethlehem alone while they return to the country of their birth, or they must themselves give up their own people to go with her, foreigners to a foreign land. Whatever the choice, it will be a life-altering one.

Orpah turns back to Moab, chooses to remain what she has always been, returns to the world in which she grew. The decision is a worthy one. It is the world for which she has been formed, after all. She knows the rules of the place. She has fit them once and can fit them again. She belongs.

Orpah's decision may not be an exciting one, but it is an understandable one. She has status to be claimed in Moab, limited as it may be. She has security there, too. If she does what that world expects her to do — marry again, be a good Moabite, keep the carousel turning — the world will provide for her what she has a right to expect in exchange: protection, honor, and the support without which her very life is in danger. What's more, she will have the satisfaction of being a "good woman," a "nice girl," a "fine citizen." It is an obvious choice, a highly moral one, a clearly transparent one, the undeniably correct social one, a traditionally spiritual one.

Ruth, on the other hand, finds herself in the throes of spiritual babel. There is no one clear voice in her. There are at least two. She finds herself pitted against herself. The easy answers aren't easy anymore. Somewhere along the line, something once taken for granted has moved in her. All the givens — that she is first and foremost a Moabite, that she is meant to marry, that she has responsibilities elsewhere, that her God is Chemosh, not Yahweh — come into question.

Ruth has been everything a woman should be — and everything a woman should not be. She has been dutiful wife, faithful daughter-in-law, good Moabite woman. The only thing she has not been, apparently, is completely herself. She has followed the rules — someone else's rules — all her life. But now she sees another life and hears another God. Now she finds herself plunged into the middle of mystery. Now she sees herself becoming something, someone, new. It is life's most perilous moment. It is the point at which we feel the anchor behind us dislodge and the ocean in front of us draw us in. Those we leave behind us shake their heads. Those who see us coming shake theirs, too. "Listen, go back," Naomi says. "I can't," Ruth says. And they are both right.

Life is not a mystery for those who choose well-worn paths. But life is a reeling, spinning whirligig for those who do not, for those who seek God beyond the boundaries of the past. All the absolutes come into question. All the certainties fade. All the relationships on which they once had based their hopes shudder and strain under the weight of this new woman's newness of thought and behavior.

Suddenly — it seems to have been, but probably only slowly, one idea at a time — Ruth finds herself at odds with her culture, her country, her religion and her role in life. One by one, she chooses against each of them. A Moabite, she makes the decision to go to the Jewish city of Bethlehem where race and religion will marginalize her forever. A follower of the tribal god Chemosh, she professes faith in the one God, Yahweh. A marriageable young woman, she opts for independence with another woman rather than set about finding a man to care for her. Ruth has discovered what it is to be the self that God made and nourishes and accompanies on the way.

Ruth has clearly changed her mind about what it means to be a woman in the world, about what it means to be spiritual, about what it means to have a relationship with God. Someplace, somehow she has been transformed from child to grown-up, from girl to woman, whatever the consequences. She has made up her own mind on things. She has developed for herself the set of ideas upon which she intends to stand. She has struck out on her own. She has begun to define herself rather than to allow someone else to do it for her. She has become a spiritual adult.

Who knows how such things happen? Who knows how it is that one day a woman begins to realize that life as she is expected to live it is not cut out of whole cloth? That there are things she wants to do that lie outside the boundaries of a woman's world? Was it an isolated idea from a stray conversation years before, which, rejected at first, was never really able to be dismissed? Was it years of frustration come to a boil? Was it a theology in tension with itself, the growing consciousness of a God who calls women as well as men? Was it a simple question for which there was no persuasive answer: Why can't I go to school? Why can't I be promoted? Why can't I preach? Why can't he do dishes? Why can't he watch the baby? Why? Why? Why? Or was it simply the inevitable consequence of a long, hot desire to be part of the decisions, part of the

system, part of the administration, part of an adult world that the men around her took for granted and women took as impossible? Or was it the end result of such assumptions ridiculed?

Whatever the catalyst, whatever the enzyme of sensitivity working in the human soul, the world is full now of women choosing, even in life's midstream, paths other than the ones laid out for them by the rules, the norms, the institutions in which they grew. It is a great spiritual moment to come to know that God works in us above and beyond the templates of our lives.

Transformation is that moment in the life of a woman — no matter how young, how old, how long in coming — when she begins to engineer her own life circumstances, to declare her own intentions, to state her own needs, to require the doing of her own decisions and to feel confident in the making of them. It is the moment when she moves beyond a mediated God to a God who talks directly to her heart. Transformation is the process of coming to wholeness, of growing into the skin of creation in such a way that we become more than we ever thought we could be before we realized that God was our God, too.

Ruth, a character created, we say, by the Spirit of God, in a world that says God does not want such things of women, is transformed before our eyes, becomes a full human being while we watch, aligns herself to another woman and sets off to make her way in the world confident that the God who began this journey in her will see her through to its end. And in the going, Ruth invites every woman in the world into transformation, too. It is the spirituality of transformation that brings a woman finally to the fullness of God in life. It is a frightening but a necessary journey for a woman if she is ever to be the person a creating God really means a woman — the separate, unique, ever becoming woman — to be.

Chapter Four Aging

THEY RETURN TO THE CITY OF BETHLEHEM. THE HOME OF NAOMI. THEIR ARRIVAL SETS THE TOWN ASTIR.

Ruth 1:19-21   So the two of them went on until they came to Bethlehem. When they came to Bethlehem, the whole town was stirred because of them; and the women said, "Is this Naomi?"

She said to them, "Call me no longer Naomi, call me Mara, for the Almighty has dealt bitterly with me. I went away full, but the LORD has brought me back empty; why call me Naomi when the LORD has dealt harshly with me, and the Almighty has brought calamity upon me?"

The moment we become conscious that we are no longer young, we become an even more valuable resource to other women in our lives than we ever were before. Without Naomi — her wisdom, her strength, her determination — Ruth was nothing but a possibility waiting to happen. It is Naomi who walked her through life. It is Naomi who showed her the God of becomings. It is Naomi who showed her that life was to be shaped, not simply endured. It is Naomi who taught her how to deal with a world that had little inkling to deal with women at all.

In a modern world where what a person produces is key to who they are, where function is central and jobs are few, and where over half the population is under the age of fifteen, there is a subtle but clear social stigma that comes with getting older. When physical strength declines in a society that prizes physical activity, the spiritual values that come only with the passage of time are easily slighted. For women, the problem is especially acute.

When the children have left the home and "motherhood" ends, when the physical sap that gave her status, shaped her role, her purpose, her life, dries up, a woman's place in the universe so easily becomes shrouded in platitudes but unclear in value. Even women in corporate U.S.A. hold less than 12 percent of its executive positions.[5] Leadership, it seems, is not considered to be a characteristic of females, however effective their domestic management. As a result, servant to everyone and sought out by few, a woman's temptation as the years go by is to turn more and more inside herself, her wealth of wisdom overlooked, her theology disparaged, her questions discounted, her suggestions ignored. Sometimes even derided. Often diminished.

It can be a frantic time, a desperate time of life for a woman. Time to dye the hair and buy the anti-wrinkle creams. Time to shorten the skirts and increase the makeup. Time to pretend to be something we are not. Men, who have made the physical a woman's preeminent value, too often still call us "the girls" and waiters in good restaurants call us "Miss." All of them pretend to go along with the thin disguises, of course. All of them smile a bit as they do. It makes the "girls" feel good, they say, as if being a Barbie Doll is a woman's goal in life, a stage that, once passed, must never be noted for fear the game would be up. For fear we would all have admitted then that sexuality is a woman's one hope for reckoning. It is a sorry end for that half of the human race which has shaped the souls of generations. It is an ignominious erasure of wisdom never passed on, not because it was never garnered, but because — unlike the men of the society who regularly spend their last years sitting emeritus on institution boards or pursued as consultants and civic leaders — it was never sought.

In the Book of Ruth, Naomi is acutely aware of the situation facing her now that she is an old woman alone in the world. Taken to Moab by her husband when Bethlehem was barren of food, the entire family becomes barren in Moab. The husband dies, the sons, too, and Naomi herself, beyond child-bearing years, is — the sages say in Ruth Rabba — *va-tishaer*, "left-over."[6] Of what good is she now? Now that her womb has gone dry, what other value could she possibly have that a society would seek her out, hold her up, honor her presence, encourage her voice, mark her words?

After years of absence, a lifetime of hard work, great sorrow, and a long journey, the women at the gates of Bethlehem are shocked at the very sight of her. "Don't call me Naomi" — which means "pleasant," she says. "Call me Mara" — which means "bitterness" — "because the Almighty has dealt harshly with me." The remarks are often taken as a sign that Naomi is angry with God for her fate, is in despair, has lost faith. But it is just as plausible to conclude that Naomi's distress comes not from disillusionment with God directly but

from disillusionment with a world that calls itself godly and then throws old women away. That God allows such things is plain; that God wills them is not. Surely a woman knows that the words are as much a question as they are a conclusion: "The Lord has done this to me? The Lord?" Who can possibly believe that the God who created the whole human race "in God's image" so disdains one half of it?

Down deep Naomi knows, it seems, that it is precisely her "bitterness," the learnings of this older woman's life, with which we all must deal if we are ever to be a really holy people. Naomi knows that she has done what youth has yet to show itself able to do: She has grown and changed and lost and prevailed. She has outlived the worst the world could do to her and, in her last years, took another turn in life alone. She is poor and destitute of resources and striving yet. She is alive and living, despite the odds. And she has no intention of quitting, of giving up, of ceasing to live, of failing to grow. She is the sign of the whole woman whose God beckons beyond the boundaries of any age, beyond the barriers of any roles.

We talk a great deal these days about "human development" but, if truth be known, we have really understood very little of it. Most research done on the subject has, until recently, focused on infant and toddler growth. Infant development we have plotted in months. We know the very week infants should sit up, should make sounds, should be able to focus their eyes. But the aging process — its strengths and challenges, its adaptations and insights — we have virtually ignored. Almost nothing, in fact, was done in earlier protocols to chart human dynamics after the age of 45, a stage of life that has been lengthening in the Western world with every passing decade.

Instead, we have focused on youth and highlighted youth and idolized youth and dismissed almost entirely for in-depth consideration the values that come only with the process of living. What's worse, early texts called the age of 45 "the meeting of past and future," the point at which people came to terms with who they were because, it was now clear, there was no time, no possibility of being anything else.[7] Age became our enemy rather than the reservoir of our life lessons, the harvest of faith, gathered by some for the good of the many.

Whatever the progress of the physical sciences, the psychological and social dimensions of the second half of life are still to be reckoned with. Only recently have we begun to understand that life continues to develop all the way to the grave, not only physically, yes, but mentally, too. We have overlooked entirely

the fact that age is a wellspring of development, not only of spirituality, without doubt, but psychologically as well. All of life is a learning process, and only the elderly can tell us what is yet for us to learn.[8]

There is a wealth in age gained only by the living of it. Only those who have routinely left and lost parts of life and gone on living can show the rest of the world that what the world calls unsurvivable — humiliation, scarcity, failure, loss — can, indeed, be survived. And often for the best.

There are lessons that come with age that come no other way. Age is a mirror of the knowledge of God. Age teaches that time is precious, that companionship is better than wealth, that sitting can be as much a spiritual discipline as running marathons, that thinking is superior to doing, that learning is eternal, that things go to dust, that adult toys wear thin with time, that only what is within us — good music, fine reading, great art, thoughtful conversation, faith, and God — remains. When our mountain climbing days are over, the elderly know, these are the things that will chart the setting of our suns and walk us to our graves. All the doings will wash away; all the being will emerge.

Yet, of all the people unheard from in our society, it is still the older woman whose voice is missing most. We do not know nearly what we need to know about what it takes to go through the transition years from being merely "mother" to woman. We have marked menopause as a kind of crucial climax in life, a loss of ripeness, a kind of weakness, but we have not asked women nearly often enough, perhaps, what the strengths are that menopause brings to women, as well. We have marked it as deficiency rather than development, and called the conclusions "scientific" despite the fact that we had little or no data to support them. We have not wanted to hear, to collect, to catalogue the remedies that women have discovered for the common cold, the yearly flu, the children's fears, or the debilitating arthritis that never stopped them for a day in spite of modern medicine's inability to cure any of them. We have not asked them what they have listened for — hoped to hear — in the decision-making parleys of men and never heard. Nor have we asked what they've known to be missing in the human enterprise but were never allowed to contribute, or felt in their hearts when "reason" failed but were never given credit for. We have not sought what they knew about God and were never given the right to say as the documents were written and the dogmas defined and the elders, few or none of them women, sat at the gate. The spiritual insight of women, that other faith

perspective on the world, is missing, and we are all the poorer for it.

Measured by the long line of history, we have asked women almost nothing at all at any age and even less so when they got older. And we ask very little yet. A world of wisdom passes us by with the passing of every old woman but, with the world becoming more violent every day, we seldom, if ever, have the sense to mourn the loss of the secrets they take with them to the grave about endurance, negotiation, or love in the face of conflict. We never deny, of course, that women have brains, but we depend on them far too little. My mother died at the age of eighty-one, an undereducated but extremely intelligent woman who lived in the twilight of Alzheimer's disease for twenty-eight years. I have often wondered how much of the disease was hastened by the underutilization of her once fine mind. We would not ignore the development of muscles, but we regularly ignore the development of women's minds.

No doubt about it, older, wiser, closer to God, Naomi is very different now. She stands at the gates of Bethlehem, a refugee from a foreign land, a homecomer at the end of a long, long journey, a woman who has seen life as few of the women who meet her there have seen it. Weary from the burdens of her life, aware of how vulnerable she is as a woman alone in a society of families, but intent on living still, Naomi refuses to give up. She is a sign of womanly wisdom, a spiritual guide, an antidote to ageism. She stands at the gates of the city of Bethlehem, newly returned to the place of her birth, broadly experienced and immensely wiser than her peers. She has known death and gone on living. She has been struck down and refused to quit. She has looked square into the face of a bleak future and determined to shape it herself. She has challenged God as did the patriarchs before her and come back from an emotional grave as proof to the rest of us that God is not a noun, God is a verb.

The other women at the gate do not recognize her, the story points out, and the metaphor is clear: Life gives us each a different face. It is in the mien of the old that we see most clearly the truths that elevate life to fullness of dignity. It is what we bring to the edge of life from within ourselves that measures its quality.

Railing and raging, pushing and claiming, scratching and climbing we come to the peak of our physical years, but it is what we know about life, about God, about what's worth it and what's not, about what's holy and what's not, when our bodies have lost their tensile strength and our legs have lost their timber that may be what the world needs most. When we learn that lesson, as a society, as women, Naomi will have done her part to bring God to humanity, humanity to humankind, and the spiritual gifts of women to the world.

Chapter Five Independence

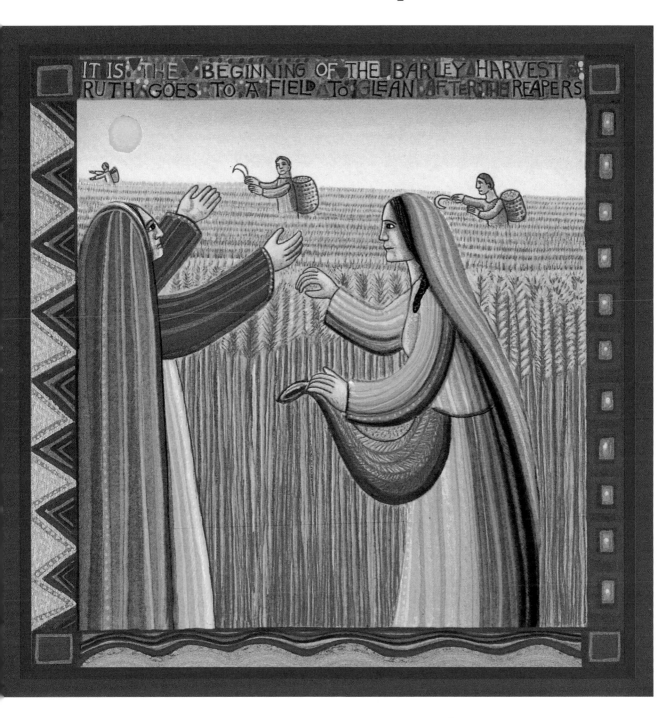

IT IS THE BEGINNING OF THE BARLEY HARVEST RUTH GOES TO A FIELD TO GLEAN AFTER THE REAPERS

Ruth 1:22, 2:1-2   So Naomi returned together with Ruth the Moabite, her daughter-in-law, who came back with her from the country of Moab. They came to Bethlehem at the beginning of the barley harvest.

Now Naomi had a kinsman on her husband's side, a prominent rich man, of the family of Elimelech, whose name was Boaz.

And Ruth the Moabite said to Naomi, "Let me go to the field and glean among the ears of grain, behind someone in whose sight I may find favor." She said to her, "Go, my daughter."

The moment a woman makes an independent decision, she becomes a real person and a spiritual adult. For Naomi and Ruth, independence is their only recourse. And, they teach us, it must be ours as well if we are ever to be, as they were, gifts to the community around us.

Everyone, if truth were known, is beholden to someone, and some of us to many. Yet, the notion of shaping our own lives, of being our own keepers, stays alive in us and dies hard, if ever. It seeps into the soul, this notion of self-direction, one small atom of thought at a time, from early childhood on and becomes, in that quiet center of ourselves, the secret standard of our adulthood, the final measure we use to prove to ourselves our maturity, our right to be alive.

It is a priceless thing, this feeling of self-direction in an infinitely interconnected world. How else can we swim against the current in the anonymous stream? "Get a good education, Joan," my mother said over and over again. "You must always be ready to take care of yourself," she insisted, because she herself, of course, could not. But it was a pitiable instruction, I realize now, a feeble voice, in a world where the notion of a woman taking care of herself was as much moral scandal as economic impossibility. Nevertheless, she knew the truth of what it meant to be a person despite that fact that woman-persons, women who were fully functioning adults, were not in much demand, whatever our theologies of creation.

Perhaps the search for independence springs from the primitive human idea that somehow or other, in each of us, there is the stuff of wholeness, however connected we understand ourselves to be to the world around us. It is a clear theological truism. We know ourselves to be distinct words of the divine. We know ourselves to be solely responsible for who we become. We know ourselves to be separate even in community. "We come into life naked and alone," the proverb teaches, "and we leave it the same way: naked and alone." We are responsible for our own souls, a woman knows, but she also has reason to wonder, given the course of history, given the structures and statistical data of the world, if she will ever actually be fully responsible for anything at all.

If I can become my own compass, the heart seems to realize, then I will be truly a person. It is a spiritually high-risk situation that teeters between narcissism and accountability, between self-centeredness and God-centeredness. Too much independence and I become my own god. Too much dependence and I stay a child forever. It is a very tenuous situation, true, but surely worth the risk. For unless a person has a real sense of self, that little impulse of the divine called conscience, a person has nothing to give away but service. And service is no substitute whatsoever for the self. Independence is the psychological grail of the Western world, discrepant sometimes, exaggerated often, but important to a development of the soul, the person, nevertheless.

It is not easy to be independent, however. Nor is it necessarily comfortable. It well may be that independence exacts a price far out of proportion to its promises. In the end, surely, it requires more personal responsibility than it gives personal freedom. And yet the grasping for the self, free and entire, never ends. For any of us.

If the Book of Ruth says anything to our time, it is about a woman's claim to independence, to be a freely functioning person rather than a thing. Ruth, the alien, the minority, "the woman of color" in a Jewish world, faces a stony environment with small chance of besting it. She is an ethnic outsider, a widow, a woman alone. In the final analysis, she has little upon which to rely but a strong sense of self, the virtue of bravado, and the magnet in her heart that drew her with relentless might toward the Creator's will for all creation, herself included.

The situation is a vulnerable one, as first attempts at dealing with life alone so often are. She has nothing much to hope for here in a foreign land and a great deal to fear: racial slurs, ostracism, and always, always, the men in the field. She has stepped outside all her woman's boundaries alone, with little hope for the future and less help in the present except for an old woman at home who loves her. It's a sad scenario that cries out for a Prince Charming to save her. But Ruth is not seeking a Prince Charming.

Ruth goes out to work after years of being housebound. After a life of housewifery — of baking bread and washing clothes and cleaning vegetables — Ruth earns her living by picking up scraps left by harvesters for the poor. And Ruth works faster than the regular field hands. She tries harder. She saves every piece of wheat in her path. She braves the sun in the field and lasts the entire day. She confronts the world on its own terms and wins. Ruth asks no favors and courts no benefactors. Ruth makes it on her own. It is a rare and shining moment. It has more to do with the dawning of the soul than it does with the gathering of grain. Ruth stands before God now a discrete individual who is determined to be everything she can be. It is the beginning of any human being's relationship with God. Until we take life into our own hands, we are at best candidates for piety, not pursuers of sanctity.

The pious participate in rituals designed to protect them from the world. The holy go beyond the rituals to wrestle with the angels of life.

True independence is a state of soul given to few men and almost no women, but without it genuine interdependence — the kind of mutual give and take that strengthens everyone involved — is impossible. Without doubt, there's something about the thought of dependence that seduces us all. Men, whatever their natural claims to the public world, are more likely to gravitate toward jobs in company towns and with corporate benefits than they are to strike out as entrepreneurs. The temptation to be secure, to be taken care of is a psychological seduction of no small consequence for any of us but most of all, perhaps, for women.

Women have been taught so well to give up their very selves in return for a false security. Where a woman is concerned, the thought of being dependent raises all the fairy tale images ever written of precious princesses and knights in armor, all of which make clear a woman's place in life. The social ideal of female dependence feeds into the notions of male mastery that keep the notion of a public-private world intact. As if every private act were not also a public one. As if what happens in a home is not the result of what happens in our legislatures and so is very much in need of a woman's voice. As if giving up ourselves to the designs of another were not the antithesis of the revelation that comes from the creation of individuals. God created all of us uniquely — and expects us to be unique.

Indeed, the notion of female dependence conjures up the old images of what makes up the perfect life: the working father and the stay-at-home mother with the full-size dollhouse in which to live — an abstraction common nowhere in the world except in the West, and even there only rarely now. But the promises continue to entice, nevertheless; the vision of being queen of the manor remains the ideal even though the promise eludes us on all sides. Few of us have the luxury of being carried through life. We either make it on our own or we don't. We have what it takes to survive or we don't. Either we can support ourselves or we can't. No doubt about it: independence is a burden of immense proportions.

Independence demands so much from a person and in the end gives very little. Except, of course, the self. And it is for the sake of the coming of the self that women seek it. As long as we have yet to know that we are capable of sustaining ourselves, as long as we are economically dependent on others, as long as we are psychologically dependent on someone else for our ideas, our ideals, our convictions, we do not yet belong to ourselves. But until we belong to ourselves our real openness to the will of God is at best more good intention than possibility. Without a healthy sense of independence, we may well know what we need to do but never have the strength to bring ourselves to do it.

But becoming independent is not easy for a woman. She is, like Ruth, the Moabite, the eternal outsider in the system. Every time a woman goes into a corporate system, she goes, like Ruth, into a foreign field. Little in the way of flex hours for parenting here. Few day care programs for children here. No equal pay here. Only golf courses and private clubs and secretarial pools, all devised years ago to meet the needs of a male workforce, not a female one. And yet, somehow, women go back into the fray over and over again because to get to be a person in a person's world is, in the end, somehow — whatever the inequities — worth it. In the end it has something to do with the very purpose of creation, of being able to go on becoming, of being able to make choices rather than simply to bear burdens.

Like Ruth, women the world over go on gleaning, picking up the scraps left behind in the field so that at the end of the day they can say to themselves, like Ruth, "We'll eat tonight." It is a mat-

ter of survival, of course. But it is also more than that. It is a matter of saying, as well, "I can do it" and "I did it myself." It is a matter of the meaning of the self. It is about having moral presence, spiritual agency, in the larger world. It is about being fully human, about using the mind as well as the body. It is a matter of visibility. It is a matter of being a self-sustaining adult. It is a matter of being fully human. It is a matter of knowing that God made all of us in the image of a God whose presence changes things.

The price of independence is no small one, true. It carries with it always the fear of functioning in the unfamiliar and the possibility of failure. But its gains are inestimable, too. For women around the world who are destined to go from the care of one man to another all their lives — from their fathers, to their husbands, to their sons — to be beholden to them and defined by them and directed by them, however benignly, independence is an elixir like no other. It is the way of saying to the world, "I am a person, too, and I am fully alive." It is the acknowledgment, as well, that I, too, am God's grace and gift for the world. I have something to do here that engages all of me, not just part of me.

Independence is the road to the recognition of the God-self in the self. Out of it comes confidence and self-esteem, self-control and self-development, self-worth and self-awareness. And in the end, far, far more than self comes, good as that awareness may always be. In the end, from independence comes the right and obligation to be a God-gift to the world, to take my own place in it, to bear it up, to make it better, to do it well.

Independence is not a woman's synonym for narcissism. It is a woman's claim to the kind of responsibility that makes her a contributing citizen of the world, a person with a mission, a lover of life, an agent in her own salvation, a wisdom figure in an unwise world, another image of God — all the things we are accustomed to finding in the men in our lives. Until a person is independent, real community is impossible. Where half the human race is not enabled to be fully contributing members of the human community, only conformity, only sacrifice is possible. Independence gives a person a right to opt into the creation of community, not the responsibility to be used by the community for its own ends only. Independence, ironically, is the only true voucher we have to true interdependence.

The Book of Ruth is about two women who take their world upon themselves, not to divide it or to escape it — they have no intention of rejecting men. Not to destroy it or deride it — they have no intention of creating for themselves a separatist system. They want only, as women everywhere want, to participate in life as adults not children, as givers not takers.

Ruth calls women to be everything they can be, whatever the odds, whatever the world thinks otherwise. Ruth goes out into strange fields alone — and takes all the women of the world with her, not simply for their sakes alone, but for the sake of the whole world.

Chapter Six Respect

THE FIELD BELONGS TO BOAZ, KINSMAN OF NAOMI.
BOAZ ASKS HIS SERVANT WHO RUTH IS.

Ruth 2:5-9   Then Boaz said to his servant who was in charge of the reapers, "To whom does this young woman belong?"

The servant who was in charge of the reapers answered, "She is the Moabite who came back with Naomi from the country of Moab. She said, 'Please, let me glean and gather among the sheaves behind the reapers.' So she came, and she has been on her feet from early this morning until now, without resting even for a moment." Then Boaz said to Ruth, "Now listen, my daughter, do not go to glean in another field or leave this one, but keep close to my young women.

Keep your eyes on the field that is being reaped, and follow behind them. I have ordered the young men not to bother you. If you get thirsty, go to the vessels and drink from what the young men have drawn."

The moment a woman realizes that she is finally respected for who she is in herself, rather than because she is some man's daughter, some man's wife, she discovers a well of possibility within herself from which the rest of the world can then draw with confidence. Ruth levels the playing field between rich and poor, men and women, not by wheeling deals or kowtowing to the mighty, not by simpering and whining, not by playing a damsel in distress, but by having the kind of character that people of character can recognize and must respect. Ruth carries the dignity of creation within her and brings everyone around her to see it, too.

To be indulged is one thing; to be recognized and respected is entirely another. Isolated women, the new norm in a system in which a growing number of laws require the admission of women to previously male conclaves, are commonly affirmed. They are coddled and attended to condescendingly. They are handled with propriety and pampered. They are noticed, even singled out for public view sometimes, applauded usually, and then often promptly discounted as a real factor in any real decisions. Little changes to mark their presence. They do not find themselves on the powerful committees of the institution. They do not become part of the administration's inner circle. They are simply there: to-

kens of a casteless class meant to satisfy the aliens at the gate without endangering the old guard. Yet no amount of tokenism — no single successful woman here, no one unusual appointment there — satisfies for the deprivation of an entire class until the entire class can expect justice and respect. Nevertheless, tokenism can be mightily effective: We ourselves, eager to fit in and get along, say less and less on the inside of the system about the inclusion of women than we ever did on the outside. We begin to talk about being "patient." We begin to argue that "change takes time." We are one of the boys now.

Minority members of establishment systems, in general, are seldom inclined to rock the boat that got them where they want to be. They are not, they are quick to point out, "single agenda people." New women members of male arenas, for instance, are often given to explaining carefully that they "were never oppressed." And then they, too, having paid homage to the promotion of women, are now properly neutralized, safe, invisible in the system. They draft few pieces of legislation aimed to better the condition of women, they nominate few women to join their ranks, they enlist few women consultants, counselors, and support staff. It is a pernicious thing, this gain of place without benefit of respect. And we are all prey to it. We all sell our souls a bit to be seen as "reasonable" people, as "nice" feminists, as good, God-fearing religious women. But real spirituality goes the way of the wind when being "nice" becomes more important than being true to what's true, clear about what's right, committed to what's of God around us — whatever the pressures we face in the doing of it.

There is, of course, as much reverence for women in the world as there is rejection. But reverence comes far too often at far too high a price to pay: nice women do what the system expects them to do. They learn to murmur and dither and serve at the court of propriety, to do things "nicely," to be "objective," to be "logical." They know "a woman's place" and they keep it. And the world runs well that way. Roles are gender assigned. Power falls to one gender, sacrifice to the other. No need to say which is which. No need to balance the agendas of the world at all if order is more important than justice, if reverence is more important than respect.

Clearly, a woman's real problem lies just as much in being too revered as it does in being too reviled. To be revered means to meet the expectations of those who really have respect in a society. To be revered means, then, to be allowed to be only half of who you are. It is not a simple choice: To be what other people want you to be gets approval. "I'm not a feminist but . . ." I said for years, eager to keep my credentials as "good sister," "nice woman." Then one day I noticed that I was for equal pay, equal rights, equal representation, equal protection under the law, and a theology as respectful of women as channels of grace as it was of men. There was no way out. I could no longer exclude myself from the ranks of those who believed in the full implications of the fact that women were also rays of God's energy on earth. "I don't want you anyplace near my daughter," a woman said to me. "I want her to be a good wife and mother, not a feminist." As if the two are irreconcilable. But the situation was clear: To be what you are, to say what you think, to do what you need to do to be your most developed self means to risk rejection. The remnants of that kind of social mentality lurk everywhere yet. Little girls still are told to be "little ladies," meaning docile and quiet when they may most need to learn to be assertive and loud. Adolescent girls still get catcalled down one street and up another. Adult women still leave marriages after years of disapproval, and they still leave churches, too, after hearing throughout their entire lives that even God has rejected them. The problem becomes how to keep self-respect in a society that claims to revere you but does not respect you.

The Book of Ruth, on the other

hand — ancient, overlooked — is an interesting study in self-reliance and self-respect. And this from the hand of God. Ruth, the Hebrew Scripture is clear, is a widow long accustomed to the social roles ascribed to women, to foreigners. She is a Moabite — the worst of outsiders in the Jewish culture in which she finds herself. But with great sense of self, she simply claims its rights. "I'm going into the fields," she says (Ruth 2:2). I'm going into a man's world, in other words, because I have a license to be there. She's a resident alien and a widow but she has rights and she knows it. She is entitled by Jewish law to the leftovers in the field, and the field owners are required by the same law to see that something is left for gleaners. Clearly, Ruth comes seeking justice, not favors. She doesn't slink around the edges of the place. She makes no apology for her existence. She doesn't scratch for crumbs at the end of the day. She applies directly to the overseer at the beginning of the work day and she stays there all day long. She is a gleaner and she gleans.

When Boaz catches sight of the strange woman and asks the question, "To whom does she belong?" the answer is a clear one. Ruth belongs to no one but Ruth. She is not a wife, not a slave, not betrothed. She is on her own and clearly more than capable of it. Then, comes the miracle in the scene. The response she gets for being who she is and doing what she needs to do is respect. Ruth is a woman to be reckoned with. And Boaz does. He gives her water out of the buckets drawn by his hired hands in a culture where foreigners were more likely to be slaves than citizens, where women were owned, and where it was women who drew water for men, not men for women.

Clearly, the Word of God in the Book of Ruth is that women have rights, that women are strong and capable creatures, that women are independent human beings, and that God respects women. It is a far cry from either reverence or rejection.

Respect is not the fine art of being socially proper. A woman is respected when she's taken seriously, when she's listened to, when she's afforded the intellectual attention that being an agent of God demands for every human being. Women, too, are a Word of God and as a Word of God are also worthy of being heard.

What we revere, on the other hand, we idolize and encase in our own expectations of it. We don't need to listen to people of whom we make idols because we already know what it is that we honor about them.

What we revile we dismiss as unworthy of us. We don't listen to people we revile because we already know that nothing they say is of any real value. What we revile we seek only to control. But what we respect we hear.

The people we respect we allow to have points of view of their own. We look to their opinions, in fact, in order to evaluate our own. We discuss their comments and explore their ideas and seek out their perceptions for fear we have missed something of merit in the course of our own deliberations. What we respect we seek out for our own sakes.

The woman who's respected never needs to cry or beg or nag to get her way. She grows to full stature as a participating adult — and we with her and because of her. Both she and we know that such insight is a gift of God. Legal equality is no substitute for respect, as every woman knows who is hired but overlooked for promotion, who is educated but whose ideas are ignored in a conversation, who is driven from the field to which she has legal right but little social support. Indeed, equality does not bring respect. On the contrary. Respect is the foundation of equality.

God is Ruth's claim to equality, and Ruth is God's sign of respect for women.

Chapter Seven Recognition

BOAZ ON FINDING RUTH IS A KINSWOMAN OF NAOMI, OFFERS HER HIS FIELDS FOR HER TO GLEAN. SHE IS GRATEFUL.

Ruth 2:10-17   Then she fell prostrate, with her face to the ground, and said to him, "Why have I found favor in your sight, that you should take notice of me, when I am a foreigner?"

But Boaz answered her, "All that you have done for your mother-in-law since the death of your husband has been fully told me, and how you left your father and mother and your native land and came to a people that you did not know before.

May the LORD reward you for your deeds, and may you have a full reward from the LORD, the God of Israel, under whose wings you have come for refuge!"

Then she said, "May I continue to find favor in your sight, my lord, for you have comforted me and spoken kindly to your servant, even though I am not one of your servants."

At mealtime Boaz said to her, "Come here, and eat some of this bread, and dip your morsel in the sour wine." So she sat beside the reapers, and he heaped up for her some parched grain. She ate until she was satisfied, and she had some left over.

When she got up to glean, Boaz instructed his young men, "Let her glean even among the standing sheaves, and do not reproach her.

You must also pull out some handfuls for her from the bundles, and leave them for her to glean, and do not rebuke her." So she gleaned in the field until evening. Then she beat out what she had gleaned, and it was about an ephah of barley.

The moment a woman achieves something on her own efforts and is recognized for it publicly, the whole vision of what it is to be a woman changes, not just for her, but for the rest of the world as well. When Boaz recognizes Ruth for the quality of her work and the values in her life, every woman — every man — takes a new step into a new kind of humanity. They become human beings together — she as well as he.

The situation is too seldom so, even in what seems to be the best of circumstances. When Elizabeth Dole was seeking to be nominated the Republican candidate for the 2000 U.S. presidential race, *The New York Times* published an article on its editorial page wondering how it was that Bob Dole, her spouse and a former presidential candidate himself, could comment that he was Elizabeth Dole's "biggest fan and supporter" and then start talking about writing a check to a senator who was running against Mrs. Dole. Bob Dole was, he then added as if the two events were totally unrelated, looking for "ways to help [Senator John] McCain in particular." On the other hand, the article went on to note, Elizabeth Dole had been her husband's most fervent and unflagging supporter.[9] Bob Dole's statement stuns for its blatant insensitivity but not for its content. The world has long preferred

men to women, whatever God's clear acknowledgment of both as full human beings.

As women we have long known what it is to be competent and at the same time invisible. In fact, invisibility has been made into a virtue as a well as a social role for a woman. The Word of God in a woman was neither an awaited nor an anticipated addition to the world. The inconspicuous, unobtrusive, woman — the support staff of the world — is the popular image, the social ideal. But the implications are plain: What we don't see we don't need to reckon with, and what we don't reckon with we don't see. The effects have serious consequences surely, both for society in general and for women and men themselves.

The truth is that recognition is the flame that warms the center of every heart. Every child in a family struggles to be singled out, to be noticed, to be loved for themselves alone, to be affirmed for the sheer uniqueness of their existence. Teams and companies and institutions everywhere thrive on buttons and ribbons, on trophies and insignia, on the public proof of their achievements — however minor, however parochial, however mundane. Recognition is society's way of telling people that they are valued, that their work is necessary, that their efforts are honored, that their life has been noticed.

To withhold recognition is to withhold the oxygen of the soul. But we do it routinely where women are concerned. When a man cooks, he's a chef; when a woman cooks, she's a cook. When a man joins a company as an agent, he expects to move quickly into a supervisory position, into a higher income bracket, into management. When a woman joins a company, she stays in the secretarial pool until she retires. When men do something, it makes headlines in the daily paper. When women do something — work for years to develop the local garden club, give their lives to organizing children's book clubs, spend a lifetime on phones scheduling drivers for "Meals on Wheels" — it is far more likely noted, at best, in the thank-you column of the local church bulletin.

The effect of attitudes like this take a toll on society itself, however much unnoticed. Women's projects go routinely unfunded. Women's volunteerism goes repeatedly unmarked. Women's spiritual gifts go regularly undefined. Women's talents get overlooked. Woman's domestic work goes uncounted in the GNP, and so the widow who worked in the home all her life is left with half a social security check. Indeed, the essential obscurity of women is built solidly into the system. But what of the Holy Spirit here, then? Is there a geography of grace? Is God less available to

Ruth than to Boaz? And if so, how is it that in the Book of Ruth God works primarily through Ruth and Naomi, not through Boaz, to bring new life to the line of David from which the Messiah is to come?

Men lead, women support, we insist. But not in the Book of Ruth. Here we have a completely different view of God's ways with women. Here women do the work of God, and good men, deeply spiritual men, recognize it.

The recognition question is a key one in Ruth, just as it is in every human heart. "Why have you found favor with me?" Ruth asks Boaz. The question is no formality. Its undercurrents are sharp. Why do you accept me? the question implies. Why have you singled me out? Why have you given me privileges here? Why have you recognized me of all people, the outcast, the foreigner, the woman? Ruth wants to know. The question makes her point: She has not come pressing for favors. She is not attempting to wheedle her way into patronage. She simply wants her due.

Boaz's answer is as clear and direct as her question. "Because I recognize the good you do." In other words, I know that you are hardworking, capable, competent and worthy and I want it noted. No sexual game playing here. No groundless beneficence. No grandstanding by Boaz. No Bob Dole he.

He does not make political statements in one sentence and retract them in the next. No, Boaz recognizes Ruth in a special way — accent on "recognizes" — because she deserves it in a special way. By the end of the day, Ruth had gathered an ephah, a basket, of grain. An ephah we are told is equal to twenty-nine U.S. pounds today. The ration of food that a working man of the period would be given rarely exceeded two pounds a day.[10] Ruth had gathered in one gleaning the equivalent of half a month's wages. Ruth was not a worthless worker, a welfare queen, a beggar bent on seducing the system. Ruth was independent, enterprising, energetic, committed, and faithful. And Boaz, just, honest, and secure man that he was, recognized it, honored it, and instructed his staff to do likewise.

Boaz singled out a woman for praise in a world that barely noticed women at all, that listed women with cattle and slaves. Boaz didn't manipulate the system in her behalf. She shaped the system to her advantage and he gave her the regard she deserved. Her recognition came as a result of her achievements. It is a social situation devoutly to be wished.

Recognition is a necessary dimension of human development. It is the offspring of the theology of creation. What God did, God recognized as good.

What we do as co-creators of the universe to make this world a decent, better place deserves to be recognized as well. Without it we smother the part of the human being that strives to be most human and most godlike at the same time. Without recognition we have no measure of our worth, no mark of our growth. To work without valuation and recognition is to work in the dark with blinders on. To be recognized is a sign that I am alive and that someone else has seen the godlike gift and the human beauty of it. Recognition calls me to sense the Spirit everywhere — and respond.

If is possible, of course, to work for the sake of working. Animals do. But that is not human. Humans work because work is a reflection of the divine in them. Humans work to be creative. To have that work ignored, as women's work has been discounted for centuries because they have been pronounced inferior — or now equal but "different" and therefore inferior — is not only an affront to creation. It also is a barrier to creativity. The world is all the poorer for the denigrating of women's work. To belittle the work of a woman because it is done by a woman is to dismiss the value of half the human race. But if one-half the human race is weak, the other half is weakened.

To withhold recognition is a deep sign of insecurity on the part of those

who see but will not recognize another person's value. It is so much easier to ignore what we cannot better than it is to compete with it. Ruth earned half a month's sustenance in a single day. And the Word of God made a note of it. Here was no weakling, no whiner. Here was a woman stronger than what the theologians who come after her said she was, made of sterner stuff than the philosophers to come said she was, capable of finer things than systems everywhere said she was. Here was a woman.

The great spiritual question now is: When will this be taken as the norm? When will all the false comparisons of women with men ever end? "She thinks just like a man," we say, as if being a woman weren't enough. And, saddest of all, we sincerely mean it to be a compliment. But all it is, in reality, is one more indication that women as women have yet to be really recognized for what they are as women, for what they bring as women, for what women in themselves — and unlike any other — bring to the human race, for what God has given women as women. Women are not pale shadows of men. They are unique, discrete creations of God with gifts of God to go on giving.

"Why do you favor me? Ruth asked Boaz directly. "Because I recognize the good you do," Boaz answered. Such recognition of a woman by a man is surely the Holy Spirit's answer to the use of Scripture to justify the heresy of the hierarchy of creation. God willing, this Word, too, may someday be fulfilled.

Chapter Eight Insight

RUTH BRINGS TO NAOMI THE GRAINS SHE HAS GLEAED NAOMI RECOGNIZES BOAZ AS HER KINSMAN

Ruth 2:18-23   She picked up [the ephah] and came into the town, and her mother-in-law saw how much she had gleaned. Then she took out and gave her what was left over after she herself had been satisfied.

Her mother-in-law said to her, "Where did you glean today? And where have you worked? Blessed be the man who took notice of you." So she told her mother-in-law with whom she had worked, and said, "The name of the man with whom I worked today is Boaz."

Then Naomi said to her daughter-in-law, "Blessed be he by the LORD, whose kindness has not forsaken the living or the dead!" Naomi also said to her, "The man is a relative of ours, one of our nearest kin."

Then Ruth the Moabite said, "He even said to me, 'Stay close by my servants, until they have finished all my harvest.'"

Naomi said to Ruth, her daughter-in-law, "It is better, my daughter, that you go out with his young women, otherwise you might be bothered in another field."

So she stayed close to the young women of Boaz, gleaning until the end of the barley and wheat harvests; and she lived with her mother-in-law.

The moment a woman understands that all men are not worthy of her simply because they are attracted to her she becomes worthier herself. Naomi knew the differences between the two kinds of men and did not hesitate to say so. What she wanted for Ruth was not a male breadwinner. She wanted a man. She wanted someone who was worthy of Ruth's womanhood, someone who could deal with it without having to diminish either one of them to do it.

But diminish women we so often do. It's hard to know how it happens, but the process is progressive and inexorable, however well intentioned. First a female child is only a name and the color pink — to signal her softness. Then, she's a "little girl" — as in "little girls don't." Then, she is simply a girl, skinny, gangly, giggly, betwixt and between, who is lured into thinking of herself as more physical than intellectual by every advertisement in every storefront in town. And then, one day, suddenly, she's a woman. Ironically, every stage carries with it less and less freedom, more and more restrictions. "Be a lady," "That's not womanly," and "Be careful now" are the hallmarks of a sex-defined system.

"You shouldn't be over in that field playing with those boys now that you're thirteen," my father said about a field I'd already been playing in for five years. I was bewildered. But that was before I understood the illogical logic of it all. It took years before I realized that he knew something about men that I did not. It took years for me to realize that whatever the apparent gains for women in the public arena, fathers still know that their daughters need to be warned against trusting themselves to strange fields. And therein lies the spiritual problem for both men and women.

The whole thing, this construction of the woman's role out of completely different cloth, is indeed a mystery. But it is not entirely the woman's mystery alone. Being a woman has every bit as much spiritually to do with what it means to be a man as it does with what it really means for us to be feminine.

Becoming conscious of her womanhood is an essential moment in a woman's development, but it is not complete until she becomes just as conscious of what really constitutes the fullness of manhood, as well. Both images have been distorted over time. Both ideas are often left more to billboards and Hollywood to describe than they are to human insight, to spiritual reflection. As a result, the images we inherit of what it means to be a woman or a man, masculine or feminine, are no more flattering to men than they are to women.

Women have been conditioned to become seductive females, men violent and sex-hungry predators. Women have been presented as victims, men as victimizers. It's a pathetically partial definition of both. It erases depth of soul and leaves only a shell for either women or men to grow into as they go. We both suffer a loss of self in the separation that wounds us throughout life.

Incomplete understandings of what it means to be a woman or a man, such as the Tarzan and Jane tradition, are abject to the ultimate. As a result, we get women in their 50s who lie about their age and men in their 40s who know how to fight but who do not know how to cry. We get a plastic world full of winners and losers rather than a holy world full of holy people. We get a gossamer kind of piety. We get the trappings of religion designed to simulate the roles and structures of the world around it, when — given a fuller understanding of gender, of humanity, of spirituality — we would develop, perhaps, a more prophetic voice.

Just as some women are not women but little girls dressed up pretending they are adults, some men are not men either. Not really. They are often macho. They may even be masculine. But until they are secure enough in themselves to deal justly, equally, and intellectually with women, they are not men. They are simply pale imitations of the real thing, afraid of being bested, fearful of losing

control, incapable of admitting their limitations, and bent on distorting the Scriptures to prove it.

When a man makes a woman in a man's group feel like a traveler in a foreign land, when he dismisses or minimizes what she considers important, when he seeks the response only of the other men in the conversation, most of whose standards are white, male, Western — with everything those categories imply — that man has yet to have reached manhood. He is posturing — either for the sake of swagger itself or for other men just as underdeveloped as he is.

There comes a moment in every woman's life when each of us has to learn to distinguish between men who are spiritually whole and men who are not. The problem for a woman comes when she assumes that every man is worthwhile or, just as bad, that no man is worthwhile. The danger is to confuse one kind of man with the other. The Book of Ruth calls us all to develop the insight it takes to tell one from the other, for the sake of both men and women.

Naomi, the older woman, more experienced and, at the same time, more wizened by her wounds, makes the point quite obvious. She knows about men what Ruth does not: that all of them do not yet know that women are the other face of God, not lesser versions of themselves made simply for their use.

On her first day in the field, at the very outset of her insertion into the public world of men, Ruth meets both kinds of men. Boaz, Naomi points out, is a distant relative, family, one of us, "a kinsman of ours," Naomi says. It's an important lesson. Ruth has happened into safe territory, in other words, into the presence of a man of honor who recognizes the value of a woman. He treats her as an equal, as a Jewess, rather than as Moabite, as inferior, as outsider. He doesn't ignore her. He doesn't exploit her. He doesn't ridicule her. He doesn't attempt to control her. He simply suggests that she work in his fields, next to his women servants, rather than roam other fields alone. Then he uses his services to empower her services. Naomi understands immediately: "Stay there with the women," she says to Ruth, "and don't go into other fields where" — earlier translations of the story say quite clearly — "you might be molested." The line is drawn quite plainly: With some men she is not safe. With this man, she is. There is a distinction to be made that takes insight.

Ruth comes face to face here with what it means to be a woman in the presence of men whose manliness has been prostituted for the sake of machoism, men for whom manliness has been warped to mean domination or brutishness and women who have been made to be things. The tradition has, tragically, honored both: "Women should be brought up," the philosopher Nietzsche wrote, "as a plaything for soldiers."[11] But Ruth clearly knows herself to be more than what the philosophers of hierarchy have said that women are. And in Boaz, she finds that men can be more than what machoism says they are, too.

Boaz is a real man. He helps make the world safe for everyone, including women, in a world that preys on women and uses them badly with few to notice and fewer to care. He notices Ruth. He sees the quality in her. And he sets out to do his part in honoring it. He takes Ruth into his inner circle; he talks to her as an equal. It's not a love affair, a mating game, that's being played out here; it's a covenant between equals based on the relative gifts of each and the *hesed,* the loving-kindness, of the God who made both to reflect the glories of the divine. It is Ruth and Boaz together who make the will of God happen in the Book of Ruth. Just as it is only women and men working together who can make the will of God happen here and now. Just as it is only women and men together who can reflect an integrated image of God.

If Naomi is the female Job of the Hebrew Scripture, the one whom "God has struck with God's own hand," then Boaz is surely the figure of the God who blesses the beauty of all creation and basks in the presence of women as well as of men. To fail to realize that there are such men who respond to women in justice and respect them as equals is to miss the whole point of feminist spirituality: We can all be more than the warped connotations of both men and women that culture, tradition, society, philosophy, and a theology of hierarchy have allowed us to be.

The Book of Ruth says that we can all be more than what a sexist world paints us to be. We can be women with male strength and men with a feminine sensitivity. The Book of Ruth says that it is not the responsibility of women to be a civilizing influence on men; it is the responsibility of men to be civilized.

The temptation, of course, is to wonder, in the face of so much sexual oppression, if the equality of creation is really possible, if men can really come to recognize the full humanity of women. But that is precisely the pitfall Naomi wants Ruth to avoid. To see sexism everywhere, to see sexism only, as feminine consciousness begins to break through in us is to run the risk of stamping out our own wholeness before it can possibly come to life.

The spiritual life is a life grounded in an attempt to fulfill the will of God for creation. What we say we believe, if we are truly spiritual persons, we make real, we make present. To assume that God made women in God's own image and then to discount their spiritual value, their human wholeness, is to distort spirituality itself. To know that God made men to share life with women and then to assume that men are constitutionally incapable of living and working with them equally is to deny the will of God. It is to distort the spiritual life itself.

Man-hating, the paranoia that makes every man a foe, is the chief enemy of a woman's own development. It blocks the coming of the new world because it fails to realize that feminism is not a female thing; it is a human thing. It fails to see that patriarchy is not a male thing — men are not inherently oppressors — it is a systemic thing. It fails to see that patriarchy is a system that is structured to oppress women and debase men, to distort the full image of God in both of us, no matter how benignly.

Until women and men together begin to realize that sexist systems, systems that limit the living of life because of gender definitions, are as destructive of men as they are of women, both men and women will continue to be diminished. Until men and women together see that any sexist system is destructive of both sexes, there is no hope of cauterizing the disease that oppresses one sex on the basis of gender and pretends to privilege the other one on the basis of natural right but in truth destroys both. By putting unattainable, unreasonable, and unhealthy goals in front of both men and women — by turning men into work machines only and women into sex objects primarily — it deprives them both of the fullness of human and spiritual development. Worse, it makes real spirituality, authentic spirituality, impossible.

In a sexist system, women find themselves arrested intellectually; men find themselves crippled emotionally. "You don't need an education," they say to her. "You'll have a man to take care of you," they argue, while her mind lies fallow and the world is deprived of half its resources. "Real men don't admit to women that they're afraid," they say to him while his life goes to dust for want of understanding. Both of them, as a result, stay caged inside themselves.

It is insight into the differences of spirit that Naomi wants for Ruth, and it is only insight that can save us still. As women, we must have the insight to value ourselves wholly before we can possibly require others to value the whole of us as well. We must redefine for ourselves what it is to be woman. A woman must discover that to be a

woman is to be more than a female. To be a woman is to be a thinker with a heart, a seer with an alternative vision. To be a woman is to carry both the future of the world and the best of the tradition within us, to hold life in our hands, to form and shape the world out of an ethics of care. We must take our place as voice for the other agendas of the human race. We must develop the insight to realize, too, that men aren't real men when they set out to own and control the other half of the human race. We must own the feminine in God and the Spirit of God in ourselves.

We need, as both Naomi and Boaz teach us, to quit glorifying, to stop tolerating, the kind of man who is not a whole man. We must also cease to tolerate any presentation of women that is not womanly, that is not adult, that is not fully developed. Then women will have the chance to be whole women. Then both men and women can be more together than they can possibly be alone. Then the glory of God will shine in both for both to see.

Chapter Nine Empowerment

NAOMI TELLS RUTH TO WASH, ANOINT AND DRESS HERSELF,
THEN TO PRESENT HERSELF AS BOAZ SLEEPS AT NIGHT

Ruth 3:1-5   Naomi her mother-in-law said to her, "My daughter, I need to seek some security for you, so that it may be well with you. Now here is our kinsman Boaz, with whose young women you have been working. See, he is winnowing barley tonight at the threshing floor.

Now wash and anoint yourself, and put on your best clothes and go down to the threshing floor; but do not make yourself known to the man until he has finished eating and drinking. When he lies down, observe the place where he lies; then, go and uncover his feet and lie down; and he will tell you what to do."

She said to her, "All that you tell me I will do."

The moment a woman becomes conscious of the way her world goes together, she is obligated to say her truth for the sake of all the women yet unborn. Then, because of her, their own lives may be better than hers was. Otherwise, her role as the other image of God is lost, and the world will see no more of it in the future than it did in the past. Women, the Book of Ruth demonstrates, must claim their part of the will of God. Naomi is such a one. Naomi is a woman who knows how life works, and, powerless as she is in the system, she has great strength of self, great consciousness of her dignity as a daughter of Rachel and Leah and Sarah. She knows herself to have a place in God's order of things. And she passes on to Ruth the kind of consciousness it takes to move the system closer to its own integrity, if only one inch at a time.

The fact is that every generation of women forms the next. What one is, the next also will be. What one begins, the other will complete. What one shrinks from facing the other will bear.

"Women don't do those things," one generation tells the one after it. "Don't make him angry, dear," one woman warns a younger one. "Whatever your husband wants is what you'll have to do," a mother tells her daughter. "Get your career started before you get married," a woman coun-

selor tells a woman student. Directions echo across the ages from woman after woman to girl after girl. What we value, they learn to value, too. What we fail to see, to consider, to articulate will take them years to discover alone. I earned the first fifty cents of my life at the age of ten. I had plans for it. But my mother took me, two quarters in hand, marched me to the bank at the corner, opened a savings account in my name, and said, "Joan, give the man one of your quarters. You must save half of everything you earn. A woman without money is a woman who cannot take care of herself." I winced when they took the quarter out of my hand, but I knew that I had grown one step closer to womanhood as a result of it.

Naomi values security, too. It is the arch ideal of her generation, the only real question for a woman of her time. And for a woman of that period, security lay only in marriage. Without it, women starved. Without it women were considered immoral. Without it, women were seen as useless. Marriage was the imperative. Women, religion taught, were saved by childbirth. After all, what else was a woman for? No doubt about it, security — marriage — is a must for Ruth. Of course Naomi values it.

But Naomi values Ruth, as well. And Naomi values empowerment, as well. The daughter who is not her daughter is all that is left of her life. And

she wants the best for her. "My daughter, I need to seek some security for you so that it may be well for you." And this from a woman whose own security hung by a thread, whose own security has been shattered. But however tenuous her own situation, it is Ruth's situation that counts to her more. It is the empowerment of Ruth for which she lives. It is, in the final analysis, every woman's dream: that her daughter, that the women who come after her, will have it better than she did because she did what she could to make God's will for her possible. In this case, empowerment means finding a husband for Ruth, however daunting the task might be to make a marriage, to assure security for an alien widow in a strange land.

With the echo of the patriarchs playing under her speech, just as surely as Abraham sends Isaac looking for a wife to carry on the family, Naomi sends Ruth to find a husband. But not just any husband. Naomi wants more than security for Ruth. Naomi wants good for Ruth. Naomi has toward Ruth the *hesed,* the loving-kindness of God. They are to one another *hesed,* the loving hand of God in one another's lives. Against all the odds, Naomi wants Ruth in the hands of someone who will value her as Naomi herself values her. She wants Ruth to marry Boaz.

Boaz is a good man. He is also one of only two remaining distant male relatives of her own deceased husband Elimelech. He is one of only two men in Bethlehem who, under Jewish law as nearest of kin, has the right to "redeem" — to buy back for the family by virtue of the laws of inheritance — that land lost to the clan when Elimelech and his heirs died. It was a serious situation. To lose the family land, to lose the family heir, the family name, is to endanger the security of the entire clan. It is to erase the family from the face of the earth. Yet to reclaim the land for the clan is one thing; to find a husband for Ruth is another. Naomi wants Boaz to marry Ruth and to redeem the land for the family, yes, but she wants him to do it for Ruth's sake most of all. Naomi is responsible for the young woman, Ruth, and she has no intention of leaving her unable to cope in the world around her.

At first blush, it can seem that the empowerment of the next generation is a fantasy. How do any of us guarantee the security of women in any society that is shaped, often on religious principles, around the needs and values and privileges of the other half of the human race? If women aren't permitted to go to school, as they are denied in so many parts of the world yet, how do we train our daughters to take care of themselves in the future? If women aren't permitted to vote, how do we train them to make public choices in their own behalf? If women aren't paid what a man is paid for doing the same kind of work, how do we enable them to save themselves from bad marriages or to feed the children of failed ones? If women are kept out of ecclesiastical enclaves, in what way can a woman's insights enrich the spiritual understandings of humanity? To send Ruth into a situation that has no room for her is to doom her to failure before she even tries. But Naomi knows, as well, what every woman alive knows. Unless we take risks in our time, the time to come will be no better for the women who depend on us now to make the path. What is more, the world itself will be no more whole, no more human, no closer to the mind of God in times to come than it is now in an environment that still breathes dualism and domination, no matter how benign.

Indeed, Naomi knows very clearly the problems Ruth faces in her search for security. Ruth is a Moabite, a foreigner, an outcaste, a widow; Boaz is one of the best-placed men in town — older, wealthy, an honorable Jew. The social complications are obvious: there is a racial problem here; there is an age question here; there is a religious question here. There is nothing whatsoever, in terms of established social wonts, to commend such a marriage. To send Ruth to Boaz is to flaunt all the conventions of Israel. Except one: justice. Boaz has a responsibility here, a slim one some would say, but a real one nevertheless. He is not technically required to marry Ruth because she is not the widowed wife of his dead brother, the essential characteristic of the levirate marriage. But as *go'el,* as close male relative and therefore as designated redeemer of the family, he is required to look after the land of the entire clan. He has a moral responsibility to the family at large.[12] And Naomi intends to press it, not for her sake but for Ruth's.

Ruth, clearly, has become Naomi's security. But the question weighing Naomi down is what, after Naomi dies, will be Ruth's? It is the question every woman wonders when she looks into the eyes of any daughter, of any woman younger than she.

Clearly, what at first glance looks as if Naomi herself is leading Ruth into some kind of sexual sacrifice, upon closer examination taps a deeper well.

Naomi — whose name for God is *Shaddai,* the God with breasts — is taking the kind of nurturing Godlike risk that crosses racial barriers, religious stereotypes, and boundaries of male privilege. She is intent on requiring the system to contend with its obligations. And Ruth is ready for the contest. Just as Ruth went out into the fields among the male harvesters, she is now venturing into Jewish society. And on her own terms. Whatever its previous norms, she is set on breaking them.

The spiritual problem for Naomi, the older woman, then — the problem for women of this generation, too, if we really want to empower the next — is to stay alive to the world around her, to the world in which she herself was raised, and to scrutinize it carefully, to critique it unmercifully, to wrestle with it unremittingly, and somehow, somehow, to shape it to her own ends. For her sake? Not at all. For the sake of the women to come after her to whom she is leaving her world. The injustice she does not face down, she knows, she wills to them. The injustice she knows but does not name makes her complicit in it. The God she knows but does not reveal is a God not seen. To choose "spirituality," defined as the comfort that comes from escaping into private religious practices, when religion demands that we attend to the fulfillment of the mind of God in the world, is to make a mockery of both religion and spirituality.

If we make no judgment on our own lives, we cannot possibly make better the lives of those who follow us. The woman who assumes without question that what was canonical for her will be equally right for her daughters fails the next generation. The woman who knows the questions but never articu-

lates them betrays her daughters totally. The woman who experiences injustice and refuses to name it fails every girl child ever born. Our task is not to hand on old answers; our task is to gift the women who come after us with new questions. Otherwise, we run the risk of passing down to the next generation a yoke where no yoke should ever be.

The function of one era must be to build bridges to a new one. Mothers who told their daughters that to live pregnant all their lives was to be too pregnant brought the world face to face with the question of family planning. Mothers who insisted that their daughters be sent to college as well as their sons gave the world thinking women. Mothers who followed the stars inside themselves, who developed their own talents as thoughtfully as they raised their children, showed the world how to be the kind of family that does not depend on one person's life being sacrificed for the convenience of everyone else's.

The function of an older generation of women is the empowerment of the next. We have not done our duty until we teach them every lesson, give them every question, prepare them to the hilt, empower them to begin, and allow them the privilege of risk. Anything else is to leave them powerless in the face of systems made only for the powerful. Any-

thing else is to give up on the powerful, but spiritually unaware, without giving them the opportunity to live fuller, deeper, more wholesome lives themselves. Anything else is unworthy both of Naomi and of Ruth, who knew within themselves God's *hesed*, God's loving-kindness for women, too — and trusted it.

Chapter Ten Self-Definition

AS BOAZ LIES ON THE THRESHING FLOOR RUTH ASKS HIM TO TAKE HER AS HIS WIFE BOAZ TELLS RUTH THAT

Ruth 3:6-14   So she went down to the threshing floor and did just as her mother-in-law had instructed her.

When Boaz had eaten and drunk, and he was in a contented mood, he went to lie down at the end of the heap of grain. Then she came stealthily and uncovered his feet, and lay down.

At midnight the man was startled, and turned over, and there, lying at his feet, was a woman!

He said, "Who are you?" And she answered, "I am Ruth, your servant; spread your cloak over your servant, for you are next-of-kin."

He said, "May you be blessed by the LORD, my daughter; this last instance of your loyalty is better than the first; you have not gone after young men, whether poor or rich. And now, my daughter, do not be afraid, I will do for you all that you ask, for all the assembly of my people know that you are a worthy woman.

But now, though it is true that I am a near kinsman, there is another kinsman more closely related than I. Remain this night, and in the morning, if he will act as next-of-kin for you, good; let him do it. If he is not willing to act as next-of-kin for you, then, as the LORD lives, I will act as next-of-kin for you. Lie down until the morning."

So she lay at his feet until morning, but got up before one person could recognize another; for he said, "It must not be known that the woman came to the threshing floor."

The moment a woman takes action to shape her world for her own sake she comes to the point where she knows herself to be a creative force in it. Naomi and Ruth do not wait to be saved; they make it happen. They have no intention of being victims just because the society does not see them as advocates of their own lives. To become an instrument of God, a moral agent, they know, you must decide to be one.

Life is so often made up of a little of what we do see — and a great deal of what we do not. Seldom has such an awareness been more true than in the scene between Ruth and Boaz on the threshing floor. Traditional exegesis concentrates on whether or not the images used — the fact that Ruth is bathed and dressed for beauty, the mention that she lies down by Boaz, the reference to the fact that she "uncovered his feet" — is proof of some sort of sexual liaison between the two. The central questions become: Did Ruth seduce Boaz? Is that how she got him to marry her? Isn't that the age-old trick?

They are, I'm sure, authentic research issues. At the same time, they're sad and pathetic questions, not because they titillate or smirk or smack of presumption but because they so obscure what else is really at issue here. They simply perpetuate a tired patriarchal bias. They concentrate on Ruth's femaleness and miss her womanliness entirely.

Surely it is what we are not seeing in the scene that the scene on the threshing floor is really all about. This episode is at base about what it means to be powerless and forsaken, intelligent and committed at the same time. It is about what it means to take life into your own hands.

The scene is about the lives of two marginalized women who are desperate. They live in a world, not unlike most of the women in most parts of the world yet today, if we would only admit it, where a woman's single life option is marriage, whose only use is sex, and whose only long-term security lies in producing male children who, as the possessors of the age to come, will be her guarantor. If you are a woman, it's about using the sexual, all right. But it's about using the sexual to circumvent the sexist society that creates it. It is, in reality, about women using the system to annul the system.

Naomi and Ruth are the husks (Hebrew: *atvaeshar*) that remain after the men who were their lives have all died. They are women without a life: Naomi, the mother-in-law, is too old to marry again and with both sons dead has no one to care for her. Ruth, a younger woman, might well have been marriageable in her own country if she had stayed there. But as a Moabite, a member of the only people in all of Scripture whom the Torah curses, her chances of being married in Bethlehem, let alone accepted into the society, are limited indeed, if not unlikely. Clearly, when Ruth decided to stay with Naomi rather than to return to her own home, she left her future as well as her past in Moab.

There is, at the same time, one hope. Israel is a kinship society, and Naomi has family in Bethlehem, however distant. In Israel, the welfare of widows is an obligation of the clan. But nothing happens. Oh, a grain of wheat here, a cup of water there, perhaps — charity but not security, nothing permanent, nothing loving. In a society that professes a commitment to *hesed*, the loving-kindness of God, no man — not one — has come forward to help these women get stabilized, find home, despite all the kinship expectations in Israel.

The truth is disconcerting at best: If Naomi knows that Boaz is a close male relative, the one with the power to redeem the family land and support the family women, then Boaz knows it, too. But Boaz, for whatever reasons, however understandable, does nothing of substance to change the plight of these women whom male society does not treat with "loving-kindness," whatever the cry of the prophets about the rights of widows and aliens. And so the threshing floor.

It is on the threshing floor that Naomi and Ruth take the system into their own hands. They plot its capitulation. They change things in a society that says that women are not its changers and that nothing can be changed. They take the pittance of the law and use it to liberate themselves from death in a world that is death-dealing to women, however pure the world's intentions.

The women move Boaz beyond the letter of the law to the spirit of the law. Boaz agrees to redeem both the land and the women its dead owners left behind on the dung heap of humanity.

Was it a sexual ploy? Probably. After all, in a society that sees a woman in terms of her sexual value only, what other maneuver is left to a woman? The problem becomes why it is that we create societies in which sexuality is a woman's primary value and then castigate and label and punish women for using it for their own purposes. Why is it that we usually publish the names of prostitutes, for instance, but not the names of the johns who use them? Why is it that we want women in the home and then force them and their children to live beneath its established economic standards after they are divorced? Why is it that, having denied women the right to work for equal wages all their lives, we also deny them the right to their husband's full pension and social security check after he dies? Why is it that women are defined by only part of what they are? Why is it that women are denied the fullness of self-definition the world over? All of which calls itself by some set of religious standards, holy.

The message in our own times is no less pointed to us, surely, than it was to Ruth and Naomi. We will not be saved from the inequities of a gender-blind system, a system that never asks itself how its laws and customs and roles affect women and men separately, by sitting and waiting for that system to save us. Why would any system that is running nicely for the people who shape it and control it and benefit from it change? Why would a system that prospers for some at the expense, no matter how benign, of others, self-destruct? Why would plantation owners of their own accord give up their slaves? Why would corporations on their own share their profits with unions? Why would a man willingly divide the money and the household tasks equally with a woman if that meant loss of power, loss of convenience — unless, of course, there were something more authentic on the other side of the divide for everyone concerned? "When the baby comes," Karen told me, "Ted and I will each be working part-time. That way he can be home

with her in the daytime and I can be there at night. We decided that that was the only way we would have children." In an instant, I watched "motherhood" become "parenting" and fatherhood become a state of life instead of an event. I watched an old system fall and another, a better one, rise to take its place. I saw a new kind of self-definition begin to emerge. Ruth and Naomi and Boaz stretched one system to include outsiders; these two young people were changing another to make marriage an enterprise in which both parties can be whole. They were not waiting for the perfect world; they were perfecting it for themselves. Indeed, the Book of Ruth is quite plain about the situation: What any of us need for ourselves we will need to assure for ourselves. Nothing changes until we change it.

We cannot be saved by waiting for God to turn life upside down. God does not intervene with trumpet and chariot in the life we create for ourselves. In fact, God is not even really a character in the Book of Ruth. God is a reality upon whose essence, whose love, the women rely, but God is not a magic act. They do not wait for God to perform some kind of miraculous legerdemain. If God is demonstrating anything at all in Ruth, it has got to be that we all have in ourselves everything we need to reconfigure the pieces of our soul. It is simply a matter of having the courage to be everything that God has given us the gifts to be.

The miracle of Ruth is clear. It is the women themselves, it is Naomi and Ruth, who strategize their own redemption in the Book of Ruth and do it by using the very system put in place to obstruct their ability to do it. Without a doubt, God relies on humans, on us, on the apparently weakest of us, to make happen what the human heart knows deep within itself are really God's designs for the world.

Indeed, Ruth goes to the threshing floor to maneuver a future for herself and her mother-in-law. Women have been doing it for centuries, using what little the world gives them to make up for what it hasn't. God inspires them; God enables them; God blesses them for their efforts. And Ruth is in the midst of it calling them to more, always more, until the day when women, too — all women — are full human beings. The very fact that women keep striving for the fullness of humanity may be the greatest act of faith they can make in a just and loving God.

Chapter Eleven Invisibility

THERE IS ONE KINSMAN BEFORE BOAZ THAT HAS THAT RIGHT
BOAZ MEETS HIM AT THE CITY GATE THE KINSMAN BEFORE

Ruth 4:1-10   No sooner had Boaz gone up to the gate and sat down there than the next-of-kin, of whom Boaz had spoken, came passing by. So Boaz said, "Come over, friend; sit down here." And he went over and sat down.

Then Boaz took ten men of the elders of the city, and said, "Sit down here"; so they sat down. He then said to the next-of-kin, "Naomi, who has come back from the country of Moab, is selling the parcel of land that belonged to our kinsman Elimelech. So I thought I would tell you of it, and say: Buy it in the presence of those sitting here, and in the presence of the elders of my people. If you will redeem it, redeem it; but if you will not, tell me, so that I may know; for there is no one prior to you to redeem it, and I come after you." So he said, "I will redeem it."

Then Boaz said, "The day you acquire the field from the hand of Naomi, you are also acquiring Ruth the Moabite, the widow of the dead man, to maintain the dead man's name on his inheritance."

At this, the next-of-kin said, "I cannot redeem it for myself without damaging my own inheritance. Take my right of redemption yourself, for I cannot redeem it."

Now this was the custom in former times in Israel concerning redeeming and exchanging: to confirm a transaction, the one took off a sandal and gave it to the other; this was the manner of attesting in Israel.

So when the next-of-kin said to Boaz, "Acquire it for yourself," he took off his sandal.

Then Boaz said to the elders and all the people, "Today you are witnesses that I have acquired from the hand of Naomi all that belonged to Elimelech and all that belonged to Chilion and Mahlon.

I have also acquired Ruth the Moabite, the wife of Mahlon, to be my wife, to maintain the dead man's name on his inheritance, in order that the name of the dead may not be cut off from his kindred and from the gate of his native place; today you are witnesses."

The moment a woman begins to understand that her life is, in everything that really matters, completely out of her hands she finds in herself the reason to change it for others. In the Book of Ruth two women wait helplessly for the world to do justice for them. Despite the fact that they have a case, despite the fact that they have a need, they stand at the mercy of a system of which they are not a participating part. They stand silently by while others make the decisions that will most affect their own lives. And with them stands every woman shut out of every economic, political, and ecclesiastical institution in the world begging for bread, begging for voice, begging for her soul.

It is impossible to be a fully conscious woman until we begin to realize what it means to be treated like less than one. Facing their crises with character and faith, Naomi and Ruth provide a metaphor for what it means to be a woman. But the Book of Ruth also shows with dispiriting clarity an insight into the world around them. What woman even today has not known the insult of having been made invisible? Left off the ownership papers; left off the deed; left out of the deliberations; left off the bank account; left off the administrative team; left out even of the pronouns of the language?

In the fourth chapter of the Book of Ruth the situation is painfully clear: Ruth's fate gets decided by two men — out of her hearing, without her input, despite her desires. However much Ruth would prefer to be married to Boaz, another man has, according to the laws of the day, a higher claim to Ruth and the family land than Boaz does. And Boaz does what has been done from time immemorial: he honors the man's rights rather than Ruth's dreams for her own life.

Boaz, we are told over and over again across the years, is an honorable man who saves the women, a veritable figure of a redeeming God. And from one perspective, so he is. He is a good man in a bad system. But how really God-fearing is the man who is willing to accept a bad law, a female-blind system, and do nothing whatsoever to change it? To his eternal credit, Boaz uses the system to the advantage of the women, but Boaz — able as he is to manipulate the system in his favor — does not question the system itself.

The second kinsman is perfectly willing, Boaz discovers during the negotiations at the city gate, to take the land his kinship position to the deceased man allows him. He does not, however, want to take the woman of the family with it who, still marriageable, might well yet give birth to its heirs. This man clearly has no concern at all for the plight of two widows left at the mercy of a society with no place for unmarried women. So Boaz, without doubt a good and generous man, claims the prize. He wins Ruth. But he does not himself do anything, it seems, to challenge the system, to decry the law, that made women pawns in the matter of their own futures.

It is a complex and confusing situation. Good men are not to be dismissed simply because they are men. Good men are not to be brutalized, discounted, or sneered at to balance the brutalizing, the dismissal of women. One evil does not deserve another. Female chauvinism does not correct male chauvinism. Sexism is sexism whoever is a victim of gender discrimination. Good men are good. But as benign as some slaveholders surely were, it did not make slavery right. The world needs men who can see it through a woman's eyes.

Victor Hugo wrote in *Les Miserables*, "Just has its anger, and the wrath of justice is an element of progress." Women shudder at the thought, but the prophets knew the truth of it. The prophets knew that anger was a virtue. Violence and anger are not to be confused, of course, whatever the cause. Violence destroys. Violence assumes unto itself the judgment of a just God. But there is such a thing as holy anger.

There is such a thing as the anger that drives us to do right, whatever the cost to ourselves, for the sake of righteousness. Boadicea, the first-century British queen, knew it and freed prostitutes from the prisons designed by the same men who used the prostitutes in the first place. Teresa of Avila knew it and reformed religious life. Martin Luther knew it and reformed the church. The framers of the United States Constitution knew it and formed a new nation. Mother Jones knew it and started the Knights of Labor to save the poor from profit mongers. Harriet Tubman knew it and risked her life to guide slaves to freedom. Sojourner Truth knew it and spoke everywhere, at whatever cost, for both the emancipation of slaves and the equality of women, white and black. Elizabeth Cady Stanton, Mary Wollenstonecraft, and Harriet Taylor knew it and defied the law to mount public protests for women's suffrage, however much they were jailed and ridiculed and driven from public places. Rosa Parks knew it, too, and simply refused to give up her seat on a segregated bus. And Ruth and Naomi knew it and set out to engineer their salvation for themselves.

Generations of women, deprived of the right to influence the documents, the decisions, that regulated their daily choices and controlled their futures — made them passive spectators of their

own lives — have known it, too. They have gone powerless from generation to generation but kept alive in their hearts, regardless of resistance, the simple question, "Are women human, too?" They asked the question to which "Yes, but . . ." is still not a good enough answer. They passed it on to their daughters, planted it in their sons, and drew attention to it at every opportunity. And little by little, over time, water wore away the rock. Really good men heard the truth, and really good men began to change things.

Women, in some places, got the vote. In some places, women got education. In some places, women got credit. In some places women got the right to self-determination. In some places women got access to the services they needed to lead a dignified life, married or not, mothers or not. But not everywhere.

In the Turkish constitution to this day, men are defined by law as "head of the family," with everything that implies in domestic decision making. In the constitution of the Republic of Ireland, to this day, it says that "woman's place is in the home." In the United States to this day, there is still no such thing as national day care or even national kindergarten. Only in May of 1999 did women receive the right to vote in the Emirate of Kuwait. In Iran, women may not

drive cars. In many places, it is still no crime for a husband to beat a wife. "He took our children and went back to Iran," the woman told me, "because in Iran the children belong to the man. I have never seen them again."

Clearly, in some places at some times, some women have come to full stature in the human community, but not all of them everywhere. And not even completely in the United States, where women are still trying to have the equality of women recognized in the Constitution itself and not subject simply to the vagaries of the laws and legislation of the day, any and all of which can be abrogated at any time.

It is also true, of course, that many women have accepted invisibility for themselves and their daughters, have done nothing to right the balance of a world tilted precipitously in favor of the male prerogatives of male power, male freedom, and male autonomy. And many generations of women have taken for granted their inherent inadequacies, their need for direction, their obligations to defer — and do so yet. They have learned the lesson of their inferiority very well. They have found their center outside themselves, in the other, in the man whom God made, the philosophers and theologians said, more rational than God made women. More competent to make objective decisions. More intelligent, broader seeing, less emotional, less easily swayed. More given to calm and sensible actions — nuclear war and genocide and slavery, apparently notwithstanding. Yet little by little, inspired by the Ruths and Naomis of every generation, more and more women and men everywhere are beginning to suspect the truth: The God who called Abraham to be patriarch of a nation called Sarah and Rachel and Leah and Ruth to be matriarchs, to form that nation in their image as well as in his.

In the meantime, we are suffering badly from the loss of Ruth at the city gates, where the public shapes its policies and decides its directions as a people. It is a model difficult to imagine. To leave half the human race — its most caring and compassionate side, they say — out of the discussions that determine the fate of the world seems insane. How can there possibly be a decent life decision made that is not based on care, on compassion, on mothering? Conspicuous for her absence in this determining chapter of the Book of Ruth, Ruth's absence brings us all to new consciousness. Where are the women? What kind of a spiritual life can we possibly have without those insights, that perspective, that experience of God? What kind of life can we have on any level — economic, political, or social — that is not as molded, as defined, by women as by men? Where is the righteous anger that will require the visibility of what God created to image God differently, which we have for too long ignored: a woman with a mind and the obligation to use it for the good  of the human race, let alone the obligation of the world to hear?

Chapter Twelve Fulfillment

TEN ELDERS OFFERS HIS RIGHT TO BOAZ. RUTH AND BOAZ MARRY. THEIR SON OBED BRINGS JOY TO NAOMI.

Ruth 4:13-17   So Boaz took Ruth and she became his wife. When they came together, the LORD made her conceive, and she bore a son.

Then the women said to Naomi, "Blessed be the LORD, who has not left you this day without next-of-kin; and may his name be renowned in Israel! He shall be to you a restorer of life and a nourisher of your old age; for your daughter-in-law who loves you, who is more to you than seven sons, has borne him."

Then Naomi took the child and laid him in her bosom, and became his nurse. The women of the neighborhood gave him a name, saying, "A son has been born to Naomi." They named him Obed; he became the father of Jesse, the father of David.

The moment a woman comes home to herself, the moment she knows that she has become a person of influence, an artist of her life, a sculptor of her universe, a person with rights and responsibilities who is respected and recognized, the resurrection of the world begins. For Naomi and Ruth and the women of Bethlehem, the new and vital posture of two women, once castaways but now creators of a whole new life, are the sign of God's power at work in all women as well as in men.

What we do as women to bring ourselves to fullness makes the world around us a fuller place as well. It is not to women only that change happens when women find fullness of life in themselves. As women develop, men find themselves freer, less burdened, more alive. Men can put down now the kind of false responsibility that leads a man either to domination or to despair. They become aware that women are people just like they are, able to care for themselves just as they do if only given the opportunity to do so, able to shape and plan and design and lead. Just as they do.

Men, loosed from the delusion of male superiority, become freer themselves to make mistakes when having to pretend to be perfect is no longer at a premium. They come to see that feeling is not non-thinking, that it is a different way of knowing, another way of thinking, a better way to live than locked inside a rationality that is irrational.

When a woman is strong and fulfilled herself, a man finds a partner with whom to share and on whom to lean. They, too, become more of the fullness of themselves than Madison Avenue or Hollywood allows "real men" to be. "She's the best lawyer in the firm," the lawyer father said of his lawyer daughter. "I wouldn't make a decision without her." That is a far cry from the days when fathers saw no reason to educate the girls in the family.

When men and women can see one another's gifts, they see other aspects of God's image, aspects they themselves cannot reflect. Then, women and men become collaborators in what it means to be human: Not one completely human and the other half human. Not one essentially perfect and the other essentially flawed. Not one the standard of the human race and the other its pale shadow.

The God of the Judeo-Christian Scriptures is very clear about the situation here. The Book of Ruth turns life upside down. It unmasks the pretenses that pose as God's will. Boaz seems, at first glance, to be the redeemer, but Boaz is, at best, simply a good and faithful servant of the system, the quintessential institution man. Boaz redeems Ruth according to the rule of the society in which they live. It is the women who are the real redeemers of the system itself. It is Naomi who goes on co-creating possibilities with her Creator God. It is she who suggests responses that lie beyond the law. It is because of her designs that their whole world becomes more whole. Ruth presses the system to its limits and beyond. Boaz is not technically bound to marry her, nor does he attempt to — until Ruth pursues more than what the law demands. Ruth and Naomi bring the system to be its best.

It is women who drive the course of this redemption, the salvation of the human race, the coming of God into the stream of humanity. Women plot the liaison between Ruth and Boaz. Women initiate the relationship. Women make plain the resolution of the issue. And, in the end, the women of Bethlehem credit Ruth with Naomi's salvation. Finally, women name the baby — a gesture unheard of anywhere else in Scripture. Then, in a final gesture, Ruth hands the baby over, not to Boaz, but to Naomi as her own. It was Naomi's journey from death to life, from foreign land to home, from homelessness to homecoming that made this new birth of a new generation possible in the midst of barrenness.

This is woman's work, the work of the matriarchs. And of God. "The Lord made her conceive," the Scripture says

quite bluntly. Boaz is literally not even in the picture, whatever the traditional historical tendency to put him there. Most of all, it is a Moabite, the lowest of the low, the woman without any status at all, out of whose line the greatest king of Israel shall come. The very people the Torah curses in one place because of their rejection of Israel in the past become through a woman its future in another. The point can hardly be any clearer: There is no one in whom God does not come to life. No one through whom God does not work. No man whose work is greater than the works of these women.

To say in the face of the Book of Ruth that women are not meant to influence the system, that God does not work through women, is groundless. To say that women are "different," and therefore unacceptable, incompletely developed, lacking in human traits common to humans, and dissatisfactory to the work of God is at best spiritual impoverishment, perhaps patent heresy. Clearly, the Book of Ruth is the story of the fulfillment of God's will for the human race. All of it. It is the story of humanity run wild with grace and vision and the presence of God. Everywhere, in everyone. In women as well as in men.

In the Book of Ruth the whole world is new again. Relationships have been righted. The outcastes have been

taken in. The lowly have been raised up. A new generation of men — represented by a boy-child — comes to inherit a cosmos where women are its co-creators. In Ruth, we get a glimpse into God's world and find that it runs just the opposite of ours.

The implications of the Ruth story for women today pale whatever assumptions, cemented by generations of custom, may still cloud their lives in any institution, in every part of the world. It is the spiritual Magna Carta of women. Ruth lives on in Hebrew Scripture to remind us that origin and destiny are not the same thing. Naomi lives on to call generation after generation of women to begin again, whatever our ages, to make life for ourselves, to refuse to wait for someone else to swoop down to make us happy, to fear nothing and risk anything that develops the dream in our own hearts, to learn to believe in ourselves as women, to find ourselves in one another and in that way to become of more value to the world around us than we have ever been before, to see ourselves as carriers of the Word of God still to be said, still to be heard.

When will the reign of God come to fulfillment? Only when the women of the world have come to theirs. And when will that be? Only when every woman takes life into her own hands, reshapes it, and hands it on to the next generation whole and entire. And when will that happen? Only when good men, the Boazs of the world, awaken to the creative presence of women and welcome them into the rest of life, the part they hold so tightly for themselves alone.

And who of us has not known Ruth? The woman who lives in a hovel, abandoned by a man, and fresh out of food stamps. The old woman, educated long before her time, who never used her degree for a day, was never asked an academic question, never served on a prestigious panel, never ran a public meeting despite the fact that she read every book she could find. The spiritual woman who is ordained but never called to a congregation or never ordained at all because "God doesn't want it," despite the fact that God is the call in every heart.

It is time, the Book of Ruth signals us, for the presence of women to cease to be an exception and begin to be the norm. Just so that women may be saved? Certainly not. The stakes are much higher than that. The presence of women — the presence of feminine values and experience — at the heart of the world and all its institutions is necessary if a human race on the brink of extinction from war, racism, starvation, and global violation is itself to be saved.

Indeed, look at this woman's story

we must. We must not dismiss it too quickly. We must contemplate whether or not it isn't really about many of the things in our own lives. We must ask ourselves whether or not we ourselves are not really dealing with many of the same things she did. But how? What is Ruth's story saying to us, here and now, about the place of God, the will of God, in a woman's life? In my life?

The Book of Ruth is about redemption, indeed, but it is as much about the redemption of Boaz and the nation, about the family and the culture, about the next generation of men and the next generation of women, about the righteousness of religion and the salvation of religiosity, about us and the disjointed world we take for granted, as it is about the redemption of Ruth and Naomi. It is a book about women helping women to break the isolation of powerlessness that affects every other man, woman, and child alive.

It is a book to be written into every woman's — every man's — spiritual life. And the book is incomplete until every woman writes the rest of it herself.

Bibliography

Atkinson, David. *The Message of Ruth.* Downers Grove, Ill.: InterVarsity Press, 1983.

Carmody, Denise Lardner. *Biblical Women: Contemporary Reflections on Scriptural Texts.* New York: Crossroad, 1988.

Collins, Gail. "The Editorial Observer." *The New York Times,* May 18, 1999, p. A30.

De Mello, Anthony, *One Minute Wisdom.* Anand, India: Gujarat Sahitya Prakash, 1985.

Hubbard, Robert L., Jr. *The Book of Ruth.* Grand Rapids: Eerdmans, 1988.

Johnson, Eric. "Issues of Modern Living." United Press International, February 24, 1999.

Kates, Judith A., and Gail Twersky Reimer, eds. *Reading Ruth: Contemporary Women Reclaim a Sacred Story.* New York: Ballantine, 1994.

Levine, Amy-Jill. "Ruth." In *The Woman's Bible Commentary,* pp. 78-84. Edited by Carol A. Newsom and Sharon H. Ringe. Louisville: Westminster/John Knox Press, 1992.

Levinson, Daniel. *The Seasons of a Man's Life.* New York: Ballantine Books, 1978.

Nietzsche, Friedrich. "Woman as Dangerous Plaything." In *History of Ideas on Woman.* Edited and translated by Rosemary Agonito. New York: G. P. Putnam's Sons, 1977.

Ozick, Cynthia. "Ruth." In *Congregation: Contemporary Writers Read the Jewish Bible.* Edited by David Rosenberg. San Diego: Harcourt Brace Jovanovich, 1987, 361-63.

Shea, Richard. *The Book of Success.* Nashville: Rutledge Hill Press, 1993.

Trible, Phyllis. *God and the Rhetoric of Sexuality.* Philadelphia: Fortress Press, 1983.

Endnotes

1. Eric Johnson, United Press International, "Issues of Modern Living," February 24, 1999, available on the Internet at living-today@send.memail.com.

2. Cynthia Ozick, "Ruth," in *Congregation: Contemporary Writers Read the Jewish Bible,* ed. David Rosenberg (San Diego: Harcourt, Brace, Jovanovich, 1987), p. 358.

3. Anthony de Mello, *One Minute Wisdom* (Anand, India: Gujarat Sahitya Prakash, 1985), p. 57.

4. John Henry Newman, as cited in *The Book of Success,* ed. Richard Shea (Nashville: Rutledge Hill Press, 1993).

5. *Fact Sheet: The 1998 Catalyst Census of Women Board of Directors of the Fortune 500* (New York: Catalyst, 1998).

6. Robert L. Hubbard, Jr., *The Book of Ruth* (Grand Rapids: Eerdmans, 1988), p. 66.

7. Daniel Levinson et al., *The Seasons of a Man's Life* (New York: Ballantine Books, 1978), pp. 192-93.

8. Sandra Blakeslee, "A Decade of Discovery Yields a Shock about the Brain," *New York Times,* October 15, 1999.

9. Gail Collins, "The Editorial Observer," *New York Times,* May 18, 1999, p. A30.

10. Hubbard, *The Book of Ruth,* p. 187.

11. Friedrich Nietzsche, "Woman as Dangerous Plaything," in *History of Ideas on Woman,* ed. and trans. Rosemary Agonito (New York: G. P. Putnam's Sons, 1977), p. 268.

12. Hubbard, *The Book of Ruth,* pp. 50-51.